PRINCETON STUDIES IN INTERNATIONAL FINANCE

No. 72, February 1992

ECONOMIC SUMMIT DECLARATIONS, 1975-1989: EXAMINING THE WRITTEN RECORD OF INTERNATIONAL COOPERATION

GEORGE M. VON FURSTENBERG

AND

JOSEPH P. DANIELS

INTERNATIONAL FINANCE SECTION

DEPARTMENT OF ECONOMICS
PRINCETON UNIVERSITY
PRINCETON, NEW JERSEY

INTERNATIONAL FINANCE SECTION
EDITORIAL STAFF

Library of Congress Cataloging-in-Publication Data

von Furstenberg, George M., 1941-
   Economic summit declarations, 1975-1989: examining the written record of international cooperation / George M. von Furstenberg and Joseph P. Daniels.
   p. cm.—(Princeton studies in international finance, ISSN 0081-8070 ; no. 72)
   Includes bibliographical references.
   ISBN 0-88165-244-X (pbk.) : $9.00
   1. International economic relations—Congresses I. Daniels, Joseph P. II. Title. III. Series.
HF1352.V66 1991
337.1—dc20   92-3756
                                                                                   CIP

Printed in the United States of America by Princeton University Press at Princeton, New Jersey

International Standard Serial Number: 0081-8070
International Standard Book Number: 0-88165-244-X
Library of Congress Catalog Card Number: 92-3756

CONTENTS

LIST OF TABLES

FIGURE

1 INTRODUCTION

Since 1975, attempts at international coordination and cooperation[1] between the major industrial countries have focused on annual economic summit meetings of their chief executives. The current participants in these meetings are the United States, Japan, Germany, France, the United Kingdom, Italy, and Canada—collectively called the Summit Seven (S-7), when represented by their heads of government, or the Group of Seven (G-7), when meeting at the financial minister level. Although international communication and collaboration is an everyday affair for officials in the executive departments and central banks of these countries, summit meetings are unique. Summits are normally the only occasions when the chief executives of the seven major industrial countries meet as a group to discuss economic policy, and they are highly visible events that produce for public scrutiny an economic declaration of the collective considerations and actions to which the participants commit their countries.

To assess the credibility of the commitments and prognostications made at these summits, judged by the degree to which they have been fulfilled, this study sifts through the economic declarations issued at the fifteen summit meetings from 1975 to 1989. Such an assessment is

---

[1] International collaboration or cooperation, on the one hand, and coordination, on the other, have been distinguished in different ways. Some political scientists distinguish collaboration from coordination on the basis of the creation of a common good versus the prevention of common harm. Stein (1982, p. 312), for instance, writes that, "regimes established to deal with the dilemma of common interests differ from those created to solve the dilemma of common aversions. The former require *collaboration*, the latter *coordination*." Economists frequently intend the reverse reference (see Kenen, 1989, pp. 11-12, and Branson, 1990, p. 60). They thus assign the terms "collaboration" or "cooperation" to information exchange designed to prevent unnecessary miscalculations (common harm) and "coordination" to activities leading toward the production of a significant change of national policies in recognition of international economic interdependence (common good).

The declarations of economic summits, however—and our study, in turn—tend not to distinguish firmly between coordination and cooperation, using at times one as an instance of the other. The 1988 Toronto declaration, for example, contains the sentence, "International cooperation involves more than coordination of macroeconomic policies" (Hajnal, 1989, pp. 364-365; all quotations from summit documents are taken from Hajnal).

difficult because the mutual commitments of countries are couched in the fuzzy language of diplomacy and state action (Ruggie, 1982, p. 380). It is hard to evaluate the significance of promises that are not directly enforceable—particularly those left intentionally vague—and to know why they are made public. If the promises and forecasts contained in summit declarations should prove to be unfathomable or largely empty, it will be difficult to view the process culminating in their declarations as setting recognized patterns around which substantive expectations can converge. The summit process will then be seen to have little significance as an institution generating explicit agreements (see Krasner, 1982, p. 186, and Keohane, 1984, p. 8).

Careful examination, however, shows that many summit undertakings have been precise enough to be verifiable. We find a total of 209 such instances in the economic declarations issued from 1975 to 1989, and we can score the degree of compliance with them even though many of the declarations were fuzzy and imposed obligations that were imprecise.

The overwhelming impression derived from the scores reported by summit, country, and issue is that governments do not play it safe. Their leaders' concern about maintaining credibility in all areas appears to be not so great as to prevent them from entering into commitments their countries are unlikely to keep. It may not be a question of commitments made in bad faith but of compliance impeded by lack of control. Thus, pledges on the use of instruments, which the government is supposed to have at its disposal, are found to be as unreliable as undertakings in the nature of forecasts or prognostications about endogenous economic events. These are undertakings that relate to outcomes without specifying supporting policies or acts of international coordination.

Commitments that are made public and then honored to a substantial degree will be credible but not necessarily newsworthy, beneficial, or important.[2] Credibility is only the precondition, not a guarantee, for

[2] Indeed, there are theoretically "many circumstances under which coordination worsens rather than improves economic performance" (Fischer, 1988, p. 39). Oudiz and Sachs (1984; 1985); Hughes Hallett (1986); Frenkel, Goldstein, and Masson (1988); Currie, Holtham, and Hughes Hallett (1989); Frankel (1990); and Ghosh and Masson (1991) consider the full scope of international coordination and whether or not coordination pays. Principals in the process usually claim that it pays, but they do not present supporting evidence or reveal their standards of appraisal.

Rogoff (1985) and Vaubel (1985) view international cooperation as involving collusion among governments that could be counterproductive by exacerbating credibility problems and shielding each country from (currency) competition. Similarly, Taylor (1985) finds that cooperative policy rules for the G-7 countries are more accommodative to

economic declarations to have an effect on the justified expectations of governments and private agents and on the confidence with which they act. Determining whether this precondition holds is an essential and hitherto neglected first step in empirical research on economic summit declarations and on similar public documents of explicit international cooperation. It shows whether the outlook or policy commitments contained in the carefully negotiated declarations *may* matter because they are credible, not that they *do* matter.

Although the verdict differs somewhat by summit and issue, we conclude that the credibility of summit undertakings must generally be rated low. The statistical work in the Appendix supports this conclusion by deriving the critical population values for average scores that are too low to refute the joint null hypotheses of "no summit ambition" and "no summit effect."[3] Although the combined scores for all summits and functional areas are statistically significant at the 5-percent or higher level, average scores in most of the nine areas and in disaggregation by country are too low to reject the joint null.

To reject this joint hypothesis, however, is not necessarily to dismiss the summit process as a whole, for it may generate other, less publicized, products. In the words of one recent economic declaration, summits "have proven an effective forum to address the issues facing the world economy, promote new ideas, and develop a common sense of purpose" (Hajnal, 1989, pp. 362-363). If this is so, summits can be useful even if they do not lead to policy commitments.

We discuss the several products of summit meetings and issues of credibility in Chapter 2. The decisions and procedures used in scoring compliance with commitments—including partial credit for those only partly met—and in interpreting and quantifying verbal, nonnumerical, commitments are explained in Chapter 3. Chapter 4 considers which issues become the subjects of commitments at summits, and why, and Chapter 5 explains the procedures used to assess the significance of the

---

inflation than noncooperative policy rules. Hoskins (1989, p. 5) also cautions that policies of international coordination "often seek to supplant markets and to avoid market discipline, risking enormous costs in terms of real economic growth and efficiency."

This study takes no position on these matters. It seeks only seeks to ascertain whether explicit coordination reflected in a public document can matter because it is credible.

[3] As conceptualized in Chapter 5 for stochastic variables, summit ambition is measured by the amount, expressed in standard deviations, by which the expected value of a variable named in a summit undertaking is to be shifted. Summit effect is the size of the impulse actually given, which is equal to the expected displacement of such a variable measured in the same way.

scores awarded for relative compliance with commitments made. The results for the fifteen annual summits from 1975 to 1989 are reported in Chapter 6. Concluding remarks are given in Chapter 7.

2 SUMMIT PRODUCTS AND ISSUES OF CREDIBILITY

The summit process can promote international collaboration at several levels, with credibility as the key to its significance, particularly if the process is seen to crest in the final declarations ratified by heads of state. Even if the entire process is driving toward these declarations, however, as has often been claimed (see Putnam and Bayne, 1987, p. 53, and Hajnal, 1989, p. xxxi), useful byproducts may be generated along the way. We shall describe several such possible byproducts before outlining the nature of the commitments in the economic declarations.

Usually at least a year in advance of a summit, an individual, known as a sherpa, is designated by each country to represent the head of its government in coordinating and directing its preparations leading up to the summit meeting. In the early stages of planning, each of the seven sherpas first ascertains what concerns his government wishes to emphasize and what issues it cares most to raise with other governments. This is done through interagency consultations and working groups, checking with principals as needed. Once agreement has been reached within a government on the directions to be taken, they are translated into the drafts and messages exchanged with other governments. Putnam and Bayne (1987, p. 53) note that some sherpas feel their preparatory activity becomes "substantively focused and precise only when participants [are] forced to confront language encapsulating alternative approaches to underlying problems." The resulting exchanges may provide each country with new information about the positions foreign governments take on existing and developing issues, which issues they desire to take up, and where they want to carry them. Mutual attunement and compromise can then develop as issues begin to be crystallized for summit debate and for drafting the declaration.

In the intensive stages of communication leading up to the summit, opportunities for mutual gain or for the mutual reduction or prevention of adverse international spillovers may be discovered. If these opportunities engage the interest of the political actors, they may widen the scope for coordination. Such benefits remain highly conjectural, however, because summit participants rarely point to or credit such discoveries. Although the accepted public rationales for concerted action are modified from time to time, changes in rhetoric do not necessarily indicate that new insights have been brought to bear on a specific, publicly announced program. Hence, it is difficult to document the discovery of new opportunities for agreement or to pinpoint their effect on policy planning in the process of international coordination.

More likely, summits may increase the degree to which governments can capitalize on "old" opportunities by overcoming political obstacles. For instance, the external support as well as peer pressure generated in conjunction with a summit may free some governments from the myopia imposed by political insecurity. The ability to stick with plans such as a sustained lowering of the inflation rate or of fiscal deficits may be enhanced to the point of bringing opportunities for national action within reach. Inside observers such as Ostry (1990, p. 12) regularly emphasize these opportunities to "get your own house in order and the international economy will take care of itself." In these instances, international coordination may help to overcome domestic political obstacles (see Atlantic Council of the United States, 1980, p. 31, and Dobson, 1991, p. 35), stiffen a government's spine, and move it to apply a decently low social discount rate in planning investments in the future welfare of its nation.

Whether such coordination is appreciated depends on the degree to which day-to-day political pressures have prevented a government from adopting the strategic positions to which it ultimately aspires, and whether international peer pressure is viewed as helpful in this regard. Opportunities for active coordination may thus be contingent on one or more governments finding themselves out of position and seeking to lower the costs of changing course and adjusting their economic policies and structures. Even if such conditions are exceptional, the contingent risk-reduction and damage-control services offered by the summit process can be stabilizing on a continuing basis.

Prominence and Credibility

The summit process can thus be beneficial in several ways at many levels. But what is most distinctive about the process is the direct involvement of heads of state, and their ability, through joint public announcements, to affect the expectations of economic actors. That ability is predicated on credibility, and credibility is derived from prior demonstrated competence and truthfulness in describing the shape of things to come.

There is no doubt that heads of state strive to be credible to each other because mutual credibility lowers transaction costs and permits more confident exchange of obligations. Putnam and Bayne (1987, pp. 5 and 88) and Kahler (1988, p. 388) have noted that the higher the level of the negotiators, the greater the costs of reneging on any

6

agreements. "That, of course, is why deals struck at the summit are inherently more credible," Putnam and Henning (1989, p. 100) have claimed. This issue cannot be settled simply by prior reasoning, however, because it is precisely those who are expected to be truthful who may be able to deceive for temporary gain.

Governments need not rate each others' credibility solely or predominantly by the extent to which each has kept its public promises; they may have private knowledge of one another's intentions and capabilities. The public, however, must evaluate announcements by drawing on general beliefs about the policymakers and the preferences, principles, capabilities, and strategies thought to guide them. Those beliefs will have been informed by observing the veracity of previous announcements in similar policy environments.

Credibility depends not only on the player but also on the issue, so one must examine exactly what has been promised and what achieved. Having a good reputation in one domain need not spell credibility in another. If the Swiss National Bank, for example, were to announce that it stands ready to support an active stimulation policy even at grave risk to the maintenance of price stability, such an announcement would probably not be credible but would, instead, presage personnel changes at the central bank. Indeed, announcements in some areas have as little effect on expectations when made by governments with strong and unshakable reputations as when made by governments known to say one thing and do another.

There are numerous books and papers on what international cooperation could achieve if it were run by this or that model and game plan; Canzoneri and Henderson (1991) provide a comprehensive assessment. Attempts to characterize what has actually followed from cooperation and how its alleged achievements have been connected to promises or actions resulting from coordination are much rarer. Dobson (1991), in giving her own expert description and summary appraisals of coordination in recent years, refers to almost all the earlier English-language publications that have attempted to judge that process and its accomplishments.

In empirical work on the problems of credibility and political incapacity, strategic issues involving time inconsistency and the absence of precommitment generally receive far less emphasis than the constraints imposed by economic technology and the political climate. According to the critical survey of the literature on policy credibility by Blackburn and Christensen (1989), this is as it should be. The area that offers the greatest scope for future research is, they say, "undoubtedly empirical" (p. 41).

7

The concept of credibility that can be linked to the gap between promise and performance is what Cukierman and Meltzer (1986) have called "average credibility." Average credibility is lower the wider the absolute difference between the targets or actions announced and the outcome expected by private agents. If the expected outcome is what actually happens on average, a performance gap translates into a credibility gap. The trouble is that average credibility as represented by the above measure can be raised both by increased effort to meet a target and by making an undertaking less ambitious. Thus, announcing an undertaking quite devoid of ambition and doing nothing to change the inertial outcome or solution for the economic variable in question would be one way of earning the highest score for average credibility: the expected performance gap between "no effort or effect promised" and "nothing done" is 0.

Although we also compare actual to promised outcomes to derive our performance scores, Chapter 5 and the Appendix explain that we do so, not in any simple way, but by making explicit reference to the degree of ambition or the range over which a variable is to be moved. As a result, the average value of the score assigned to all undertakings that are without ambition and systematic effect is expected to be 0 under our scheme, and not 1, which would be the highest value. Hence, our scoring scheme avoids the ambiguity of Cukierman and Meltzer's (1986) *average credibility*; it comes closer to their concept of *marginal credibility*.

According to Cukierman and Meltzer (1986, pp. 48-49), marginal credibility measures the effect of a unit change in the target announced for some variable on the expected value of that variable. If the actual change turns out to be a fairly stable fraction of the announced change on average, and this situation can be expected to continue, the degree of marginal credibility may be given by that fraction.

It turns out that economic declarations frequently refer to intended improvements, that is, *changes in the levels of some variables*. Their language implies that the changes are to be measured simply from the present, rather than relative to the counterfactual outcome that would be expected without coordinated action. The goal in some cases appears to be a return to the status quo ante, if matters have deteriorated since. In the case of variables known to be subject to drifts or trends, the changes tend to apply to their rates of growth or to ratios of such variables. Some useful examples are given in the next chapter, before an overview of the areas in which commitments have been made.

3 SCORING POLICY COMMITMENTS IN PRACTICE

Before characterizing summit commitments with an eye to scoring compliance, we introduce here the metric used for scoring and explain what key decisions must be made before it can be applied. Two hypothetical cases show how scores are set to indicate (1) the degree of representativeness (or "membership") of a full range of numerical values characterizing a concept and (2) the degree of compliance with accepted obligations:

(1) If the concept involved is merely descriptive of a change in a variable but not suggestive of an undertaking, a membership function will merely indicate how well any data is judged to match a particular concept of change. It is easiest to characterize the whole range of such possibilities, going from a score of –1 to +1 and back, with an example on which we are all expert, the membership of different human ages in the concept "getting old." To what degree can a person of any age claim membership in that concept so that its degree of membership can be scored?

If a child proclaims on her fourth birthday that she is "getting old," the statement will be comical, for the membership of age four in the class of such statements will be about as negative as possible (that is, –1). If a thirty-year-old issues the same lament, it will no longer be funny or deserve a negative score. Still, there may be broad agreement that turning thirty is not what "getting old" normally brings to mind. Hence, the appropriate membership score for age thirty might be around 0. If, however, a sixty- or sixty-five-year-old says the same thing, we will say that this is the "typical" person to make such a statement. Hence, the membership score for ages sixty to sixty-five in the self-referential statement "getting old" will be 1 or only a little less. It will be decidedly less than 1 at age ninety, because a ninety-year-old is normally viewed as being old, not getting old. Indeed, if a very old person, say one who is 110 years old, complains of getting old, the comical effect, with a negative score, will reemerge.

Once the basic grid has been adopted, any age can be mapped into the fuzzy concept, "getting old" by interpolation over the nonnegative range and by using symmetry to score outcomes in the negative, or contradictory, range. Technically, this process is assisted by choosing a mathematical membership function and fitting it to the points where

9

scores 0 and 1 are thought to apply. The next example, drawn from economics, shows what is involved in the choice of functional form and the form actually chosen to derive the scores reported and analyzed in this paper.

(2) Economic declarations frequently contain fuzzy obligations, and negotiators understand that the obligations imposed should not be viewed as all or nothing or black and white. Even if the relevant target or goal is numerically precise, so that we can determine clearly whether the obligation has been discharged in full, it might not be appropriate to score performance on the undiscerning legalistic or disciplinarian yes/no binary scale.[1] A continuous numerical grading scheme is required to obtain scores suitable for determining the average degree of compliance when judging the credibility of summit undertakings.

Assume, for instance, that a government commits itself publicly to a "substantial reduction" in inflation for "next" year at a time when the rate of inflation is running at 6 percent per annum. Suppose it can be inferred from various data and policy clues behind this declaration that a reduction will not be characterized as fully substantial, or deserve the maximum score of 1, unless the inflation rate falls to 4 percent or less by next year. If inflation does not fall at all (that is, it stays at 6 percent), the score for inflation will be 0; if it rises, the score will be negative. Indeed, an increase in inflation by 2 percentage points or more will, by symmetry, be scored -1.

How, then, should one score intermediate outcomes, such as inflation falling from 6 percent this year to 5 percent next year? The score derived by linear interpolation will be 0.5. The score obtained with another type of membership function evolved from the logistic function (see Zimmermann, 1991, pp. 348-350) will be less than that (that is, 0.45), because it penalizes even small deviations quite heavily, taking away more than half of the full score of 1 for falling only half short.[2] Economists, however, tend to prefer quadratic penalty functions, which penalize more heavily any given departure from the goal the farther one has already moved away from it. They will assign a score greater

---

[1] Binary evaluations of action programs are quite common. For a recent review of a scheme of discrete but multidimensional scores per event that are ultimately compacted to yield a binary evaluation of the results of economic sanctions in terms of success or failure, see von Furstenberg (1991).

[2] For a complete explanation of the nonlinear membership functions and the way they are solved, see the appendix of the authors' companion study (von Furstenberg and Daniels, 1991, pp. 298-299).

than 0.5 (that is, 0.75) to an inflation outcome of 5 percent because they will give more credit for bringing inflation down from 6 percent to 5 percent than from 5 percent to 4 percent, if 4 percent is the goal.[3]

The compromise we strike between the legalistic membership-function approach, which presses for full compliance by harshly penalizing even small deviations, and the economic approach, which rewards partial compliance by harshly penalizing large deviations, is to revert to linear interpolation. Thus, 5-percent inflation, midway between 4 and 6, will receive a score of 0.5.

If inflation "overshoots" the objective and falls below 4 percent during the period covered by a summit commitment, one other outcome can possibly earn an intermediate score such as 0.5. The target of getting inflation down to 4 percent next year can be regarded as the single most desired outcome for the near term if the presence of nominally fixed interest-rate and wage contracting in an economy has raised fears that a steeper reduction in inflation will depress economic activity. In that case, an outcome of 3-percent inflation for next year might be given a score of 0.5 on the grounds that it is just as far away from the interim ideal as is 5-percent inflation. If, however, reducing inflation to less than 4 percent during the commitment period has been viewed as an unmixed blessing, 3-percent inflation cannot score any lower than 4-percent inflation, meaning that it, too, will get the top score of 1. Any intermediate score, such as 0.5, will then be assigned to just one outcome, in this case to reducing the rate of inflation from 6 to 5 percent.[4]

Such a unique score can be interpreted in two, not necessarily mutually exclusive ways. It can indicate that a reduction of the inflation rate by 1 percentage point has a membership of 0.5 in the fuzzy concept of a "substantial reduction" in that rate. Alternatively, if we think we know what a "substantial reduction" of inflation was meant to signify numerically or if the goal of reducing the rate of inflation to 4 percent was explicitly stated and publicly characterized as the "substan-

---

[3] The squared deviation of 6 from 4 percentage points is 4, compared with 1 for the squared deviation of 5 from 4 points. Hence, only a quarter of the maximum score of 1 is lost if the outcome is 5-percent rather than 4-percent inflation, with the remaining three quarters lost if the outcome is 6 percent, that is, if it reflects no improvement.

[4] In most areas, overfulfillment appears to be an unmixed blessing. For instance, multi-year energy-conservation targets were surpassed without unwanted help from cyclical decline or other negative side effects. For this reason, we have developed our test statistics in the Appendix as if overshooting a target always receives the same (perfect) score as hitting it.

tial reduction" sought, the score of 0.5 would be interpreted as the extent to which this obligation was met. Indeed, the need to interpret the strength of obligations or the scheme for partial credit arises in connection with both the crisp and fuzzy goals contained in economic declarations. The difference between the two is that, when the goals are not numerically specific, the process of scoring jointly characterizes the membership of data in each of the goals and in the fuzzy obligations they impose. Such mapping is essential to prepare summit undertakings for accounting, monitoring, or scoring, and, ultimately, for combining the scores by country or type of issue.

Four Examples from the 1978 Bonn Summit

We are now ready to show how these procedures have been applied to summit undertakings.[5] Our first two examples involve goals that are crisp in describing the targets to be reached and the times specified for reaching them. The third and fourth examples involve commitments that are fuzzy about the goals to be achieved in a specified time frame and the distance countries are to move in the directions prescribed. In spite of their fuzziness, however, both of these latter commitments receive extreme scores, of +1 and –1, respectively. The fourth example also shows that there can be uncertainty not just about the size of an undertaking but also about the variable or variables to which the commitment may refer. These examples may help the reader decide whether the judgments and procedures employed here are likely to lead to scoring on which an assessment of credibility can reasonably be based.

(1) A U.S. Energy Commitment. The 1978 summit declaration said that the United States "will increase coal production by two-thirds [by 1985]."[6] Coal production rose from 14.08 quadrillion BTU in 1974 to 15.76 quadrillion BTU in 1977 (when production was interrupted by a coal strike), then fell to 14.91 in 1978. Had the 3.8-percent average annual rate of increase registered for 1974 through 1977, prior to the commitment to accelerate production, continued for the next seven years, coal production would have been 19.36 quadrillion BTU in 1985.

---

[5] Examples are taken from a 126-page appendix (WP 5.1) detailing the scoring of the 209 measurable commitments found in the economic summit declarations from 1975 to 1989. Requests for this copyrighted material will be filled by Professor Joseph Daniels (Department of Economics, College of Business Administration, Marquette University, Milwaukee, Wisconsin 53233) upon receipt of a formatted (IBM) diskette accompanied by a suitable self-addressed return envelope.

[6] This is the first of two commitments that can be scored independently even though they were offered as subsidiary to the principal goal of reducing oil imports.

This outcome is given a score of 0. A two-thirds increase from the 1978 level, by contrast, would have carried production to 24.85 quadrillion BTU. This outcome is given a score of 1. Actual production in 1985 was 19.33 quadrillion BTU. Therefore, the linear score is (19.33 − 19.36)/(24.85 − 19.36), or −0.005.[7]

(2) *A German Commitment to Fiscal Stimulus.* The summit declaration said that, "by the end of August [the German Delegation] will propose to the legislative bodies additional and quantitatively substantial measures up to 1 per cent of GNP. . . ." but hedged: "The order of magnitude will take account of the absorptive capacity of the capital market and the need to avoid inflationary pressures." The hedge may be viewed as rhetorical, however, for the fiscal measures were to be taken so soon after the summit that there would be little time for new data to develop that could greatly change the outlook prevailing at the summit. Furthermore, the statement referred to additional fiscal policy *measures*, not *outcomes*, that were to take effect in 1979. It did not suggest that the measures taken should be judged by their impact on the economy, but only by their impact on the budget.

Holtham's (1989, p. 156) analysis of the fiscal package implemented after the Bonn summit indicates that government expenditures increased by about 0.25 percent of GNP in 1979, while tax cuts and allowances were worth about 0.6 percent of GNP, for a total budgetary effect that year of about 0.85 percent of GNP. Although we adopt Holtham's accounting, we note that the constant-activity-budget balances for the entire public sector, which excludes the effect of cyclical fluctuations, showed an increase in the deficit equal to only 0.6 percent of GNP from 1978 to 1979 (see European Communities, 1980, p. 65.). In this instance, a null change in the budget is given a score of 0, and a package of new stimulative fiscal measures equal to 1 percent of GNP is given a score of 1. Because the actual measures appear to have amounted to 0.85 percent of GNP, the linear score is 0.850.

(3) *A Commitment to Export Restraint by Japan.* The summit declaration said that "the Government of Japan is . . . calling for moderation in exports with the aim of keeping the total volume of exports for the fiscal year of 1978 at or below the level of fiscal year 1977." Real exports were the likely objective of this undertaking. The amount of the decrease intended was not made explicit but was assumed to be

---

[7] We assume that the increase in coal production is more accurately and representatively measured in BTU than in short tons. The data used here are from the U.S. Department of Energy (1987, p. 90).

appreciable. Accordingly, Japan would have been unsuccessful if there had been no fall in real exports, and this outcome is given a score of 0. It is less clear, however, how large the decline in exports would have to have been to constitute full success (for a score of 1).

The rate of growth in real exports during fiscal year 1977 (from 1977:I to 1978:I) was 6.03 percent, and during fiscal year 1978 (from 1978:I to 1979:I), –3.68 percent. This decline in exports occurred while real GNP was growing at an annual rate of more than 5 percent, and it implies a substantial shift in the composition of aggregate demand from foreign to domestic sources. Because the undertaking was fulfilled, the score of 1 is assigned to the actual outcome.

(4) A Multi-Country Commitment to Greater Exchange-Market Stability. The summit declaration said that the participating countries must "achieve greater stability in exchange markets." As will be discussed further, although the weakness of the dollar against other major currencies may have been the prime concern, there is no language in the summit declaration that would allow one to infer specific exchange-rate targets that can be scored. Casting goals in terms of exchange-rate variability, instead, can still encompass concerns about the level of key exchange rates if, for instance, continued or increasing weakness of the dollar is understood to contribute to their instability. We therefore interpret the commitment to achieve greater stability in exchange markets in terms of the variance of daily exchange-rate changes for the currencies of the seven countries. Specifically, we take it to mean that, compared with the period between the 1977 and 1978 summits, the variance of daily exchange-rate changes was to be reduced between the currencies of the seven summit countries during the next intersummit period from 1978 to 1979.

As the first column in Table 1 shows, the average variance of daily exchange-rate changes was smaller in the period just before the 1978 Bonn summit than at any other time since June 1, 1973, shortly after the widespread adoption of floating. It would thus be unrealistic to expect much more reduction, certainly no more than 20 or 30 percent. Therefore, a further reduction by 25 percent after the Bonn summit is given a score of 1.

TABLE 1

VARIANCE OF DAILY EXCHANGE RATES FOR CONSECUTIVE PERIODS, 1973-1990
(based on percentage rates of change)

Period	Average	$/¥	$/DM	$/£	DM/£	¥/£	DM/¥	Number of Observations
6/1/73 - 11/14/75	0.292	0.185	0.456	0.169	0.356	0.285	0.478	620
11/18/75 - 6/25/76	0.262	0.026	0.084	0.280	0.345	0.308	0.088	158
6/29/76 - 5/6/77	0.204	0.071	0.086	0.326	0.522	0.396	0.122	223
5/9/77 - 7/14/78	0.193	0.230	0.278	0.251	0.172	0.271	0.189	309
7/18/78 - 6/27/79	0.316	0.578	0.358	0.341	0.192	0.386	0.283	244
7/2/79 - 6/20/80	0.370	0.490	0.330	0.420	0.304	0.687	0.490	245
6/24/80 - 7/17/81	0.427	0.420	0.559	0.448	0.376	0.516	0.449	268
7/22/81 - 6/3/82	0.448	0.553	0.606	0.594	0.339	0.470	0.292	220
6/7/82 - 5/27/83	0.375	0.568	0.408	0.389	0.258	0.398	0.185	249
5/31/83 - 6/6/84	0.241	0.199	0.370	0.284	0.218	0.270	0.184	259
6/11/84 - 5/1/85	0.464	0.222	0.671	0.897	0.218	0.507	0.286	226
5/6/85 - 5/2/86	0.656	0.494	0.780	0.960	0.370	0.754	0.399	252
5/7/86 - 6/5/87	0.398	0.464	0.569	0.391	0.392	0.400	0.256	271

continued on next page

TABLE 1
continued

Period	Average	$/¥	$/DM	$/£	DM/£	¥/£	DM/¥	Number of Observations
	From Summit Before Plaza to Summit After Louvre							
5/6/85 - 9/19/85	0.700	0.243	0.852	1.190	0.207	0.714	0.430	95
9/23/85 - 5/2/86	0.523	0.520	0.576	0.623	0.467	0.743	0.364	155
5/7/86 - 2/20/87	0.428	0.481	0.644	0.392	0.409	0.409	0.285	200
2/23/87 - 6/5/87	0.311	0.419	0.358	0.381	0.317	0.374	0.163	70
6/11/87 - 6/17/88	0.300	0.505	0.372	0.482	0.152	0.261	0.151	256
6/22/88 - 7/13/89	0.354	0.495	0.481	0.528	0.187	0.219	0.201	269
7/17/89 - 7/6/90	0.297	0.363	0.371	0.339	0.222	0.342	0.294	247

The variances of daily exchange-rate changes shown in Table 1 were calculated from the bid-price spot quotations at the close of the London market, working with nine bilateral rates.[8] The six most important of these are shown separately in the table, but the averages in the first column pertain to all nine rates (including the U.S. dollar prices of the Canadian dollar, French franc, and Italian lira). The averages are

[8] Changes in exchange rates were calculated as differences in the logarithms from trading day to trading day, excluding all days for which complete exchange-rate quotations were not available, and then multiplied by 100 to express instantaneous rates of change in percent. This procedure is appropriate if, in high-frequency data, exchange rates are a random walk, possibly with minuscule trend (compared with the size of daily variations). The calculation of changes went to the last trading day before a summit or G-5 and G-7 agreement and resumed on the first trading day after it. This was done to keep the variances of daily exchange-rate changes, which are used to measure volatility between meetings, from including any immediate effects on the level of exchange rates of the announcements at those meetings. The exchange-rate quotations used were taken from the data service DRIFACS.

16

weighted implicitly by the relative importance of each currency in international finance; the U.S. dollar figures as one of the reference currencies in six of the nine bilateral rates, the yen (¥), deutsche mark (DM), and pound sterling (£) figure three times each, and the remaining three currencies figure once each. Because the average variance of daily exchange-rate changes did not fall in the intersummit period after Bonn but, instead, increased by 64 percent over the variance in the preceding period, the score for this undertaking is –1. This extreme negative score is appropriate because the actual growth in exchange-rate instability was clearly greater than the intended reduction.

4 MACROECONOMIC DISTRESS AND THE CHOICE OF SUMMIT ISSUES

Having explained the rationale and procedures for scoring summit undertakings, we give here an overview of the commitments in the various areas and the ways in which they may have come about. Summit declarations are not rungs in a Jacob's Ladder pointing upward to continuous improvement in the economic performance of the S-7 countries. Rather than orchestrating and marshaling a cumulative process, they report on the latest economic discomforts and crises and on the measures countries resolve to take about them in the months following the meetings. Summits provide an elevated stage for national governments wishing to be seen as actively confronting current problems, and doing so jointly. They are designed to build confidence and to exchange assurances that any give and take is for the good of all. Hence, unresolved problems, revealed by the data, should pinpoint the areas in which commitments might be expected at the following summit. The data from 1974 to 1989 thus need to be examined to infer what may have prompted the particular undertakings that will be evaluated in the next chapter.

Issues Subject to Commitments at Summits

Theories have been proposed and tested about the changing degrees to which individual countries have dominated the agenda of the economic summits (see, for example, Eichengreen, 1989, and, more specifically, Bergsten, 1990, and Herz and Starbatty, 1990). Rather than trace the changing economic pressures and particular interests that can be deduced from each country's own economic data, we develop an overall picture composed by summing the information for all S-7 countries, using their GNP or GDP weights. Such a picture may help spot the issues that will be highlighted in the summit declarations under various economic circumstances. The political assumption implicit in this crude weighting is that the degree of attention given a problem is proportional to the economic size of the S-7 country or countries in which it occurs.

The principal macroeconomic concerns that countries bring to summit meetings are similar to those that move them domestically, but the weights may well be different. Inflation, unemployment, and economic growth head the list, even though inflation is attributable

18

principally to national rather than international developments and does not show a high degree of covariance among the S-7 countries, except during years dominated by energy shocks. Movements in real interest rates are more immediately and inevitably shared internationally, just as exchange-rate volatility or misalignments affect all. In addition, specifically international issues, such as unsustainable current-account imbalances, are tailor-made for the summits.

National policy matters, such as fiscal imbalances, also appear on summit agendas. The reasons for international attention may be several. Fiscal expansion in a major country is presumed to put upward pressure on real interest rates and to affect exchange rates.[1] This presumption appears to have fit the United States from 1982 to 1985 and Germany in 1990 and 1991, although other data links are conceivable (see Sachs and Wyplosz, 1984). Abrupt changes in capital and trade flows would then interfere with economic growth and stability objectives, including those of heavily indebted developing countries (see Dornbusch, 1985, and Marris, 1985). Furthermore, the external "twin" of a fiscal deficit, whether or not begotten by real appreciation of a country's currency, can give rise to an unsustainable external imbalance and to pressures for protection from foreign competition.[2] In some countries, such as Italy, large and chronic fiscal deficits may also raise the prospect of unsustainable growth in net public debt relative to GNP and may presage adverse supply-side consequences from higher inflation taxes and increased marginal tax rates (see Alesina, Prati, and Tabellini, 1990).

Unlike fiscal measures, money-supply growth is never explicitly targeted in summit undertakings. Central banks have sought to keep their distance from the summit process, the agendas of which are prepared mostly in finance ministries or treasury departments. Even the G-7 finance ministers and central bank governors, meeting as needed between summits, have concerned themselves only indirectly with money-supply growth, typically in conjunction with intervention or other means to foster exchange-rate objectives.[3]

---

[1] Reference to the original Mundell-Fleming model is frequently made to support this view. For extensions, see Dornbusch (1987) and Frenkel and Razin (1987). On global linkages between interest rates and government debt, see also Tanzi and Lutz (1990).

[2] On the persistence of the U.S. external imbalance from 1980 to 1987, and the relation between the fiscal and external deficits, see Krugman and Baldwin (1987), Hooper and Mann (1989), and Helliwell (1991).

[3] Economic declarations stop well short of making prescriptions for money-supply growth; indeed, they usually skirt any explicit reference to monetary policy. The 1987 Venice summit declaration provided a partial exception in this regard by urging that

Outside the areas of fiscal and energy policy, summit undertakings relate to broad dimensions of economic performance. These dimensions embrace ultimate objectives that matter politically, not the specific means envisaged to improve performance. Any sharp deterioration in economic conditions, no matter what its cause, is likely to trigger summit undertakings vowing to improve those conditions, thereby casting heads of government in an active, remedial role.

If summit interventions are triggered by increased popular dissatisfaction with some important aspect of economic performance, one would expect bad news about a social good to be followed by summit commitments. Table 2 provides the collective record in this regard for seven key variables arranged roughly in order of importance. These are inflation and unemployment rates, real growth and real interest rates, public indebtedness and absolute current-account balances as percentages of GNP, and an index of the relative price of crude oil. An asterisk next to a number indicates that undertakings in that area at that year's summit were sufficiently concrete to be scored.[4] It may be noted that growth rates, fiscal balances, balances of payments, and interest rates are among the five indicators singled out by the G-7 in following up on the 1987 Louvre Accord (for a more complete account of the development of indicators for surveillance in 1986 and 1987, see Frankel, 1990, pp. 122-123, and Dobson, 1991, pp. 47-49). Clearly, therefore, the recently defined indicators coincide with the areas in which summit commitments have traditionally been made.

The hypothesis that growing discomfort is followed by summit undertakings most clearly fits for real interest rates, where undertakings could be scored during the period of record-high real interest

---

"monetary policy should also support non-inflationary growth and foster stability of exchange rates," but only in quite general terms. Earlier statements on the subject tended to be even thinner. The Versailles summit declaration of 1982, for example, read: "We are determined to see that greater monetary stability and freer flows of trade and capital reinforce one another in the interest of economic growth and employment."

[4] The relation between the classification of data in order of presumed importance shown here and the classification of undertakings used in Table 5 later in this paper is obvious for (real GNP) growth, interest, and inflation rates, and for oil (energy). Undertakings shown under ratio of debt to GNP (column 5) in Table 2 correspond to those scored as fiscal adjustments in Table 5, except that fiscal stimulus promised at the 1978 Bonn summit is not indicated in Table 2. Undertakings under the ratio of current-account balance to GNP (column 6) in Table 2 correspond to those shown under demand composition and international trade in Table 5; they all relate to the reduction in current-account imbalances to be achieved in some surplus countries by stimulating domestic demand.

TABLE 2

THE MACROECONOMIC RECORD OF THE S-7 COUNTRIES COMBINED, 1974-1989
(rates of change, year over year, or annual rates, in percentages)

Year	Inflation (1)	Unemployment (2)	Real Growth (3)	Real Interest Rate (4)	Ratio of Debt to GNP (5)	Ratio of CAB to GNP (6)	Oil Price (7)
1974	14.0	3.6	0.2	1.2	n.a.	1.1	137
1975	10.6*	5.3	−0.2*	1.5	n.a.	0.9	122
1976	8.3*	5.4	4.9*	1.8	n.a.	0.6*	124
1977	8.0*	5.3	4.2*	1.1	n.a.	0.8*	126
1978	6.9*	5.0	4.7*	0.4	n.a.	1.2*	118*
1979	8.2	4.9	3.6	1.2	20.7	0.5	161*
1980	10.7*	5.5	1.4*	4.5	21.5	0.7	252*
1981	9.0*	6.3	1.9*	7.7	22.6*	0.7	254
1982	6.6*	7.7	−0.3*	8.1*	25.5	0.6	223
1983	4.9*	8.0	2.9	7.6*	28.2*	1.0	189
1984	4.2*	7.4	5.0*	8.3*	29.5*	1.7	176
1985	3.7*	7.3	3.5*	7.0	31.1*	2.1	162
1986	2.1	7.3	2.7	4.9	32.6*	2.9	87
1987	3.0	6.8	3.5*	5.0	32.4*	2.9*	100
1988	2.8*	6.2	4.6	4.6	31.7*	2.5*	80
1989	3.8*	5.7	3.3	4.0	30.6*	2.3*	91

NOTE: Aggregates and averages, where appropriate, were computed using 1987 GNP or GDP weights expressed in U.S. dollars. Asterisks indicate undertakings sufficiently concrete to be scored.

DEFINITIONS AND SOURCES BY COLUMN:

(1) Percentage change in private consumption deflator from previous year (OECD, 1990, p. 185).

(2) Unemployment rate under commonly used national definition (OECD, 1990, p. 193).

(3) Percentage change in real GNP or GDP from previous year (OECD, 1990, p. 175).

(4) Real long-term interest rate (OECD, 1989, pp. 15, 157, extended to 1989 using the method described therein).

(5) Net public debt of the government as percentage of GNP or GDP (Chouraqui, Hagemann, and Sartor, 1990, p. 21).

(6) Sum of absolute values of current-account balances of S-7 countries in current U.S. dollars in percentage of corresponding sum of GNP or GDP (OECD, 1990, p. 184, and IMF, various issues through January 1991).

(7) OECD U.S. dollar import price of crude oil divided by implicit U.S. GNP price deflator and expressed as index 1987 = 100 (OECD, 1983, p. 75, 1990, p. 153, and U.S. President, 1991, p. 290).

rates from 1982 to 1984. The second oil shock also triggered two years of extensive energy commitments in 1979 and 1980. However, the set of commitments issued at Bonn in 1978 was triggered, not by an appreciable rise in the real price of oil, say, from 1976 to 1977, but by unresolved problems resulting from the failure of the United States to allow adjustment to the first oil shock through market means. That shock had originally caused the index used here to triple from its level of 45 in 1973.

Commitments in the fiscal area are split between commitments by some countries to increase government investment or spending generally, or to cut taxes, in order to stimulate domestic demand, and commitments by other countries to do the reverse to get their government deficits under control. Emphasis on fiscal restraint tended to broaden from Bonn 1978 to Paris 1989, and it is this type of commitment to which the statistics in column 5 of Table 2 relate. The frequency with which increased fiscal restraint is promised, in good faith or bad, but in a manner sufficiently specific to be scored, grows with the increase in public indebtedness and then stays high. The same pattern can be observed in column 6 for the sum of the absolute values of the current-account balances in the closing years of the 1980s.

This pattern suggests that not only a "derivative" correction criterion, reacting to a change for the worse, but also an "integral" criterion, reacting to the continuation of undesirable outcomes, may be at work in shaping summit agendas. Derivative correction refers to leaning against adverse developments or trends soon after they have become apparent. Integral correction addresses the results of such adverse changes, intensifying efforts to reverse them as long as the damage persists. It gets to work once the storm has stopped but the house is down. An integral restoration process is most evident with regard to inflation, where any weighted-average rate in excess of 3 percent per annum appears to have put the issue on the summit agenda—except in the year 1979.

The exception in 1979 suggests why commitments one might normally expect are not always made at particular summits. In 1979, the Saudi benchmark price of crude oil was raised steeply on three occasions, which together constituted the second oil shock. On June 28, the first day of the Tokyo summit, the Organization of Petroleum Exporting Countries (OPEC) agreed to raise the price of crude oil by 24 percent to a minimum of $18 per barrel (the price actually rose to $28 by January 1980). The OPEC announcement helped to create such inflation uncertainty as to discourage concrete commitments. Except, perhaps, in the area of exchange-rate management, through which the authorities may try to reduce uncertainty by limiting volatility (which is both its cause and effect), an exceptionally high degree of uncertainty may thus discourage commitments at the summits. A gloomy and unusually uncertain economic outlook may also explain why there were no specific commitments on economic growth in 1983. The weighted-average unemployment rate reached its peak that year, but several of the S-7 countries had not yet found the troughs of their recessions by the time of the Williamsburg summit in late May, leaving growth prospects for the year ahead very much in doubt.

Overall, these simple motives appear to explain quite well the ways in which undertakings emerge from summit negotiations. The undertakings reflect attempts to stop ongoing deterioration or to reverse its results, so long as promising to do so in the near term does not appear foolhardy. Two of the motives, derivative and integral correction, are reasons for action, but exceptions may be made to avoid embarrassment; near-term prospects may be so bleak as to inhibit commitments.

Before examining undertakings relating to exchange-rate stability, one matter still requires comment. Absence of an asterisk on an issue in Table 2 does not necessarily indicate that the issue played no role at the summit that year, but only that it did not appear in the final text of the economic declaration in a manner sufficiently specific to be scored. Thus, the development of energy alternatives to crude oil was mentioned after 1980—at the 1982 Versailles summit, for instance—but nothing specific was promised. The large U.S. budget deficit was discussed at the same summit, playing even a key role in the negotiations, according to some close observers (see Herz and Starbatty, 1990, p. 19), but the Versailles declaration contained only the bland stipulation that, "in order to achieve this essential reduction of real interest rates, we will as a matter of urgency pursue prudent monetary policies and achieve greater control of budgetary deficits."

Commitments to Stabilize Exchange Rates

The first call for greater exchange-rate stability scored in this study was issued at the 1978 Bonn summit. At that time, there was intense concern that exchange-rate volatility and uncertainty could be highly detrimental to the volume and efficiency of international trade. Therefore, the reduction of exchange-rate instability around prevailing average levels, not an adjustment of those levels, was the goal emphasized in public. Later, the pursuit of exchange-rate stability was coupled with attempts to guide exchange rates into sustainable ranges. Yet, summit declarations have tended to reflect such attempts only indirectly and retrospectively, not in the form of commitments that could be scored. The 1986 Tokyo declaration, for instance, noted that, "there has been a significant shift in the pattern of exchange rates which better reflects fundamental economic conditions."

Episodes of active exchange-rate management, concentrated particularly around the 1985 G-5 Plaza Agreement and the 1987 G-6 Louvre Accord,[5] were thus organized to a considerable degree outside the summit process. Solomon (1991) has dwelt on the need to treat exchange-rate management and international cooperation as separate issues. Secretary Brady (1990, p. 5) has even stated flatly that "the G7 policy process is not fundamentally about exchange rates," although he also called the process "successful in . . . promoting exchange market stability." Nevertheless, exchange-market objectives and international policy coordination are inseparable, at least in the sense that the choice of exchange-rate regime very much influences the *demand* for international policy coordination (see Kenen, 1989).[6] A high degree of turbulence in exchange markets, in turn, might bring exchange-rate stability to the attention of the summit and the G-7.

The results reported in Table 1 may be used to test the derivative-correction hypothesis in the area of exchange rates as well. Commitments to stabilize exchange rates were sufficiently specific to be scored in 1978 at Bonn and in 1979 at Tokyo, but only the Tokyo summit followed a period of rapidly increasing exchange-rate instability. As was shown in column 1 of Table 1, the average variance rose slightly less than 0.2 percent daily between the 1977 and 1978 summits to slightly more than 0.3 percent daily between the 1978 and 1979 summits, after

[5] The G-5 countries are the G-7 countries minus Canada and Italy. Italy boycotted the G-7 Louvre meeting, making it a meeting of six finance ministers. A fascinating account of the entire period from Plaza to Louvre is given by Funabashi (1988). Reflections on its systemic significance are found in Bergsten (1990, pp. 22-23). A most thorough evaluation of attempts at exchange-rate management during this period is given in Obstfeld (1990).

[6] The systemic element in the use of an exchange-rate regime and of exchange-rate targets as surrogates for international cooperation is emphasized also in Kenen (1990) as well as in earlier writings such as Williamson and Miller (1987), Hughes Hallett, Holtham, and Hutson (1989), and Minford (1989). Hughes Hallett (1987, p. 368) wrote that, "cooperation on shared [exchange-rate] targets, whether explicitly or implicitly, . . . is a key element in coordinating policies between countries." His conclusion was based on a study of seven multi-country models that showed policies and their outcomes to be highly sensitive to the priorities or the ideal values assigned to the shared exchange-rate targets.

having shown little change earlier. In the period after the May 1985 Bonn summit and before the Plaza Agreement in September that year, the measure of exchange-rate instability rose to 0.7 percent daily. This clearly represented a peak for the floating-rate period. Volatility then fell progressively to less than half that peak value in the two succeeding years, which included the February 1987 Louvre Accord. Between the 1987 Venice and the 1990 Houston summits, exchange-rate instability remained lower than at almost any time since 1979, even though public references to the Louvre Accord and its implied target zones became increasingly rare. Issues that fade from the summit agenda thus appear to be victims of success, whether that success is attributable to accident or design.[7]

The record thus provides some support for the mundane notion that issues giving no particular and immediate discomfort are unlikely to receive sustained attention at a summit and are quickly downgraded by the G-7. The most recent statistics on exchange-rate instability, for instance, may bear little relation to what is in store for the future and to any prospective damage exchange-rate uncertainty may inflict on international trade, finance, and growth (for discussion, see Bini Smaghi, 1990). Yet, it is recent experience, not the longer-term outlook, that appears to create most concern.

All of this implies that the summit process should not be expected to conceive and incubate systemic change. The most it can be expected to contribute to fundamental reform is to provide some support for negotiations already scheduled. This it can do by pressing for decision deadlines and for the timely completion and ratification of documents once an agenda has been set elsewhere for restructuring and governing the international economic and financial system.

---

[7] Krugman (1990, p. 21) has concluded: "In retrospect, the apparent success of the G-7 at enforcing target zones after the Louvre appears to have been something of a fluke." Dobson (1991, pp. 102-118) provides a more favorable assessment of G-7 attempts to herd exchange rates into those zones.

5 SUMMIT AMBITION AND EFFECT:
STATISTICAL PROPERTIES OF SCORES

To evaluate the scores reported in the next chapter, we need information on the distribution to expect when outcomes and scores are
affected not only by the degree of effort countries make to live up to
their commitments, but by stochastic disturbances as well. Scores that
are a linear function of the degree of compliance, as are those used
here, are convenient for deriving the average scores and standard
deviations expected in a stochastic environment. Without such information, it will be difficult to test any hypotheses about the actual average
scores. Placing the actual (sample) averages of the scores assigned to
the 209 commitments (or to subgroups thereof) in a grid of expected
(population) values calculated under a range of stipulations identifies
the conditions most compatible with the observed results.[1]

The Statistics to be Derived and Their Uses

In the previous chapters, we have given examples and explained the
meanings of individual scores. A score of 0 given to an economic
outcome that was the subject of an undertaking indicates that there
was no movement toward or away from the undertaking. Economic
outcomes, however, are subject to random disturbances as well as to
policy influences. An interpretation based on sample point estimates is,
therefore, not sufficient. We must examine the theoretical distribution
of scores and use their standard deviation to determine whether any
sample average score differs significantly from 0. Because the number
of undertakings is small in many categories, obtaining statistical parameters from theoretical distributions, rather than from sample distributions, will aid in the analysis of sample-specific results.

The statistics used for testing are found to be dependent on (1) the
degree of ambition revealed in a summit undertaking, measured by the
size of the shift in the prior distribution of the target variable, and (2)
the degree to which countries may be deemed to produce the actual
summit effects to satisfy their obligations, despite an uncontrollable

[1] As this task is quite technical, some readers may wish to proceed to the results
without delay. They may skip the rest of this chapter, although they are still invited to
read the overview that follows.

26

stochastic element preventing exact fulfillment. The distribution of summit scores is thus a function of both the ambition reflected in the undertaking and the effort expended on nudging the expected outcome toward the one promised.

This double dependency can be visualized as follows. Consider a commitment that is entirely lacking in ambition to change the status quo, and assume that no effort is made to do so.[2] Then the commitment does not open up a range of ambition within which a country can expect to earn partial credit for moving toward a goal, and compliance scores can take on only one of two values, depending on the direction in which stochastic disturbances happen to go. If deviations to one side are judged to be good and to the other side bad, outcomes receiving a score of +1 will alternate randomly with outcomes receiving a score of −1, for an expected average score of 0. Hence, the standard deviation of the individual scores is 1 and that of their mean is equal to the inverse of the square root of the degrees of freedom. The latter, therefore, becomes the test statistic for the null hypothesis that the average score reflects "no summit ambition" and "no summit effect." This test statistic is used later in this study to assess the significance of average scores.

If the joint null can be rejected, we might want to know with which account of summit ambition and effect the sample statistics most closely agree. For this purpose, consider another case in which ambition and strength are again of equal strength but are not both zero. The aim is to shift the target variable by an amount equal to two standard deviations in the desired direction, say, toward lower inflation, and the effort is sufficient to secure that result in the absence of stochastic disturbances. Finally, suppose that the stochastic disturbances are normally distributed around the target value so that it is equal to the inflation rate expected with the summit effect. Under these assumptions, one would expect half the scores to be precisely 1, because there is a 50-percent chance that inflation will be found to have been reduced by at least as much as the amount promised. There will be a 50-percent chance of getting a score of less than 1, including a 2.3-percent chance of getting a negative score, if inflation should rise instead of fall in response to an extremely unfavorable random disturbance. But the lower-limit value of −1 would be exceedingly rare, for that score would

---

[2] Even an unambitious commitment that does not propose to change the most likely or modal outcome can offer assurances that substantial deviations will not be tolerated. Such a commitment can therefore provide risk-reduction services, which are ignored here.

be recorded only for outcomes four or more standard deviations above the value of the inflation rate expected with the assumed degree of effort. Hence, most score values are much closer together than in the previous case. All told, the expected value of the average score for this case would therefore be somewhat less than 1 (0.80), and the standard deviation of scores would be much smaller (0.29).

We use these and other values[3] to form a grid for matching the small-sample averages and standard deviations obtained from the 209 scores with the population values derived under specified assumptions. The matching combination is used to identify those assumptions about summit ambition and effect that best fit the data.

A Random Walk with Allowance for Policy Effects

Because the summit process moves in annual increments, its undertakings typically refer to what is to be accomplished by the time of the next summit, at which point a new determination will be made. It is thus not too restrictive to assume that a variable that is the subject of an undertaking follows a random walk that may or may not be displaced by a summit effect, c. Although c is assigned experimentally, u is a normally distributed error term with mean of 0 and standard deviation σ_u, which brings random innovations into the process:

$$x_t = x_{t-1} + c_t + u_t. \tag{1}$$

In the experiments the results of which are reported below, c is calibrated in standard units of σ_u to show how large any summit effect is assumed to be in relation to the step-ahead normal deviation in the target variable, x, from time t to $t - 1$. Let X_t denote the goal specified for the target variable in the summit declaration made at time $t - 1$. Then c_t may, of course, turn out to differ systematically from $X_t - x_{t-1}$, most often because the strength of the summit effect will be less than promised.

The first row of Table 3 shows the means and standard deviations of scores derived under the null hypothesis that c is 0, that is, that nothing is changed by the summits. In all but the first case, however, there are ambitious undertakings; countries have committed themselves to shifting the prior distribution of outcomes by one or two standard

---

[3] The values are calculated by statistical procedures mapping an outcome distribution, which may have been shifted by summit effort, into a distribution of scores, given that the values of the scores rise linearly over the range set by summit ambition. The calculations are shown in the Appendix for the combination of cases listed in Table 3.

TABLE 3

POPULATION VALUES OF THE AVERAGE SCORE AND OF THE STANDARD DEVIATION OF
SCORES (IN PARENTHESES) CALCULATED FOR HYPOTHETICAL UNDERTAKINGS OF RISING
DEGREES OF AMBITION AND EFFECT

(scores range from –1 to +1)

| | | Summit Ambition | | |
		0	$-\sigma_u$	$-2\sigma_u$
	0	0	0	0
		(1)	(0.7184)	(0.4797)
Summit Effect (c)	$-\sigma_u$		0.6097	0.4586
			(0.5548)	(0.4326)
	$-2\sigma_u$			0.8006
				(0.2919)

SOURCE: Appendix.

NOTE: "Summit ambition" is the difference between the level of the variable targeted for time t, X_t and its actual prior level, x_{t-1}. The actual effort yielding the "summit effect" is equal to c_t in equation (1) or to what the change in x from $t – 1$ to t would be in the absence of stochastic disturbances, u_t. Both summit ambition and effect are calibrated in terms of (inflation) reductions equal to specified standard deviations of u, $-\sigma_u$. The mean and standard deviation of the scores expected for the six combinations of summit ambition and effect identified above are shown in the body of the table.

deviations of the target variable σ_u in the desired direction. Now, if x is something undesirable, like inflation, but X_t is set so as to require no reduction in inflation from its level at time $t – 1$, as in the first case considered, there can be only two scores, each with a probability of one-half: +1, if x_t should fall below X_t, and –1, if the opposite should occur. The population values of the average score, A, and standard deviation, SD, are therefore 0 and 1, respectively, as was noted earlier in connection with testing the joint null hypothesis.

Corresponding values for the five other cases in Table 3 indicate that, except when c is zero, so that A is also zero, the average score, A, is greater the more ambitious the undertaking and the more completely it is fulfilled. For the standard deviation, the situation is exactly the reverse. SD falls as ambition rises, even if c is 0, and falls again the more completely the undertakings are fulfilled. Explanations follow.

The smallest mean and largest variance in Table 3 are encountered when the undertaking is merely to repeat the status quo, and nothing more is done. If the goal, X_t, is more ambitious to start with, specifying a reduction in inflation by $2\sigma_u$, for example, but c, and hence the

29

average score, has remained zero, the standard deviation of that score will be smaller. The scores will not jump abruptly from -1 to $+1$ at the point where $x_t = x_{t-1}$, but will rise gradually from one extreme to the other, passing the zero value at the "no-change" point, and this will reduce the number of scores whose absolute value is expected to be 1. When the aim is to repeat the status quo, the number of extreme scores is equal to N, the total number of observations; when the aim is to reduce inflation by $2\sigma_u$, it falls to $0.05N$, as partial fulfillment and partial failure can now be recognized over a wide range. In the positive half of this range opened up by ambitious targeting, scores will be rising linearly from 0 for the status quo, $x_t = x_{t-1}$, to 1 for complete success, $x_t = X_t = x_{t-1} - 2\sigma_u$. By symmetry, they will not fall to -1 until the inflation rate, x_t, has climbed to $x_{t-1} + 2\sigma_u$. Figure A-1 in the Appendix helps visualize the distributions of outcomes and how they are scored, thereby yielding the distribution of scores.

If undertakings are highly ambitious, shifting the prior distribution of the target variable by many standard deviations, and the strength of these undertakings is matched by the strength of the summit effects, scores substantially below 1 will be rare. Their average will thus approach 1 and their standard deviation, 0. Generally, however, we expect to be far away from such a combination, and even making the exact effort called for in an undertaking can yield scores that are far from perfect when outcomes are beset by random disturbances.

If we could determine which of the cases in Table 3 most closely resembles the combination of ambition and effect of the N summit undertakings in a particular area, we could choose the statistics appropriate for testing the significance of deviations of the sample average, a, from the population average, A, by using the formula

$$a - A = t \ (SD)/(N - 1)^{0.5}. \tag{2}$$

In particular, if $A = 0$ and $SD = 1$ because the null hypothesis of "no summit effect" is to be tested jointly with the hypothesis of "no summit ambition," the sample average, a, can simply be divided by the standard deviation of the mean, here the inverse of the square root of the degrees of freedom, $N - 1$. The result will be the value of the t-statistic that determines the significance level of the deviation from 0. For example, suppose there are only seventeen scores to average, and a significance level of 5 percent has been chosen. The critical value of t, then, will be 2.12, and the critical value of the sample average, 0.53. Hence, it is not easy to reject this joint null hypothesis with just a few observations.

We have shown that the theoretical distribution of scores and its mean and standard deviation depend on a combination of summit ambition and summit effect. These two parameters can be estimated, and we illustrate the procedure for undertakings to reduce inflation, which, at 40 percent of the total number of commitments scored, constitute by far the largest single group of undertakings.

Inflation, measured by the GNP or GDP deflator, is one of the variables forecasted for the S-7 in the semiannual *OECD Economic Outlook*, which usually appears in June or July, near the time of the summit. Inflation is forecasted for successive half years, ending with the second half of the calendar year, for a total of three half years. OECD forecasts can thus be obtained by taking the square root of the product of 1 *plus* the annualized inflation rate in each of the two adjoining half years and then taking the square root of the product of the two resulting geometric averages. This estimate is centered on developments from the last half of the summit year to the first half of the next year, to correspond with the period associated with the summit undertakings as closely as the data allow.[4]

Because the OECD forecasts of inflation and our calibration of summit undertakings were conducted independently, summit commitments to reduce inflation may sometimes prove less ambitious than reductions implied by the OECD forecasts.[5] In 67 out of 84 cases (80 percent), however, summit ambition was positive relative to the OECD

---

[4] For example, in July 1983, the OECD forecasted for Japan annualized inflation of 0.0175 percent from the first half (I) to the second half (II) of 1983, 0.0225 percent from 1983:II to 1984:I, and 0.025 percent from 1984:I to 1984:II. The square root of $1.0175(1.0225) = 1.02000$ and the square root of $1.0225(1.025) = 1.02375$. Both of these estimates contain the forecasted inflation rate from 1983:II to 1984:I. Taking the square root of $1.02000(1.02375)$ and subtracting 1 yields 2.19 percent as the estimate of the OECD forecast of inflation that can be related to the 1983 summit undertakings in this area. In most years, such undertakings related to annual rates of change in the GNP or GDP deflator from the third quarter of the summit year to the same quarter of the next calendar year. Details are provided in the authors' unpublished appendix, available upon request (see Chapter 3, note 5).

[5] Committing to something less than the improvement forecasted need be neither meaningless nor worthless. Because forecasts relate to expected values of stochastic variables, such commitments may serve to limit or insure against large negative deviations by promising counteraction should they threaten to occur.

31

forecast. Averaging over all of these commitments, ambition is therefore positive and equal to an average reduction in the annual inflation rate by 1.73 percentage points from the level forecasted by the OECD. Because the standard deviation of the actual S-7 inflation rates was 6.05 percent in the years for which summit commitments were made about them, the commitment is therefore to shift the distribution of inflation rates down by 0.3 standard deviations relative to the OECD forecast.

The average degree of ambition for the subset of 67 undertakings displaying positive ambition relative to the OECD forecast is to reduce inflation by 2.52 percentage points. The average score for those undertakings is 0.227, meaning that the effect achieved is equal to about one-fifth of the ambition.

This result is very similar to that reported in Chapter 6 for undertakings to reduce inflation, although such reductions are measured there from the most recent levels rather than those forecasted by the OECD. For the S-7 commitments analyzed in Chapter 6, the intended reduction in inflation[6] averages 2.53 percentage points, which amounts to 0.4 of the standard deviation of their inflation rates. The average score is 0.222, again indicating fulfillment by little more than one-fifth. With 84 such undertakings, this score is just barely significantly different from 0 at the 5-percent level under the joint null hypothesis of no summit ambition and effect. Under this hypothesis, the standard error of the average score would be equal to 0.110; it is the square root of a fraction equal to 1 (which is the standard deviation of scores shown in the first entry of Table 3) divided by the number of degrees of freedom (which is one less than the number of observations).

Although the linear scoring scheme credits summit undertakings on inflation with having been honored at least to a small degree, summit undertakings are not better forecasts than those of the OECD. The root mean square error (RMSE) is even slightly higher for the summit "ideal" than for the OECD forecast when both are compared with actual inflation in the period following each summit; the RMSE values are 5.10 and 4.72 percent, respectively. Hence, there is no support for the hypothesis that the inside or advance knowledge generated in the final stages of preparation for a summit would give the summit declarations an advantage over the OECD forecasts prepared somewhat

[6] Because summit participants did not usually have available the GNP/GDP deflators for the second quarter just ending or ended, the status quo on which summit undertakings were calibrated is defined in most cases as the rate of inflation from the first quarter of the year preceding a particular summit to the first quarter of the summit year.

earlier and published usually in July. In this area, at least, we find no support for the assumption that national governments are better forecasters than other technically qualified groups, including international organizations, or for the assumption that information exchange among governments is a valuable consequence of international collaboration or even its main benefit (as Humpage, 1990, has asserted, based on his review of the literature).

6 RESULTS FOR THE ECONOMIC SUMMITS FROM 1975 TO 1989

As explained in Chapter 5, sample averages are needed to assess the predictive accuracy, and hence credibility, of summit commitments. Furthermore, the greater the number of scores averaged, the more conclusive that statistic can become. By the same token, summit commitments differ not only by occasion, country, and economic area, with promises of change necessarily tailored to the circumstances and prospects of each country, but by the importance that summit participants attach to issues from case to case. Hence, averaging also has its limits.

The compromise chosen here in reporting and analyzing scores for undertakings similar to those in Table 2 is to present both overall averages and averages for particular groups. First, simple averages and an experimentally weighted set of averages are shown for each of the fifteen summits. Then, scores are combined by summit but separated by either country or issue.

In almost any summary evaluation of multiple dimensions of performance, scores tend to be averaged over measures referring to different capabilities. The context will determine whether an average is intended to give a reading on a complex factor-loading of attributes or to record the mean outcome of repeated tries. Obviously, one must average apples and oranges in some way if the question is about the average number of calories a person has obtained from fruit. In the same way, the heterogeneity of summit undertakings scored is not troublesome if the purpose of score averages is to throw light on the singular issue of credibility. It is commonly observed that truthfulness can be established quite well by observing how potential partners act in little things, not just in big things. The degree of truthfulness can carry over from one issue to another because it pertains to the character of the actor or the process, not just to a particular event.

Scores by Summit

Simple and weighted averages of linear scores are shown for each of the first fifteen summits in Table 4. Application of the experimental weighting scheme involves three steps: (1) The average score received by each of the S-7 countries on its individual ("single-country") undertakings is weighted by the proportion of that country's 1980 GNP (or

TABLE 4

SIMPLE- AND WEIGHTED-AVERAGE SCORES FOR THE FIRST FIFTEEN SUMMITS
(*population values of standard deviations in parentheses*)

Summit	Date	Number of Scores	Simple Average	Weighted Average[a]
Rambouillet	11/75	9	0.408 (0.669)	0.566
San Juan	6/76	16	0.351 (0.575)	0.306
London I	5/77	10	0.381 (0.596)	0.093
Bonn I	7/78	26	0.343 (0.693)	0.386
Tokyo I	6/79	15	0.623 (0.640)	0.791
Venice I	6/80	14	0.159 (0.610)	0.035
Ottawa	7/81	12	0.266 (0.815)	0.234
Versailles	6/82	15	0.823 (0.316)	0.852
Williamsburg	5/83	19	0.066 (0.662)	−0.104
London II	6/84	20	0.352 (0.578)	0.426
Bonn II	5/85	14	0.200 (0.674)	−0.014
Tokyo II	6/86	4	0.765 (0.237)	0.592
Venice II	6/87	8	0.857 (0.259)	0.938
Toronto	6/88	14	−0.450 (0.628)	−0.580
Paris	7/89	13	0.187 (0.701)	0.109
All Combined		209	0.317 (0.688)	0.280

SOURCE: Unpublished appendix available from authors (see Chapter 3, note 5).

[a] The country weights, corresponding to the seven countries' dollar-valued 1980 GDP, are 0.423 for the United States, 0.164 for Japan, 0.127 for Germany, 0.103 for France, 0.072 for the United Kingdom, 0.070 for Italy, and 0.041 for Canada.

GDP) to the 1980 GNP (or GDP) of all the S-7 countries combined. If all countries have not engaged in single-country commitments at a particular summit, weights are scaled to sum to 1 for those that have. Combining these weighted scores, we obtain the weighted-average score for all the single-country undertakings made at a particular summit, with the weights reflecting the importance of the country making the commitment. (2) The proportions of all single-country and multi-country undertakings made at a particular summit are used to weight (a) the weighted-average score derived by (1), and (b) the average score obtained for all multi-country commitments. (3) The sum of (a) and (b), so weighted, is the overall weighted-average score for a particular summit. The weighted-average score deviates from the simple-average score unsystematically, depending mostly on the extent to which the average score for the largest country, the United States, differs from those for the other S-7 countries.

Table 4 shows that the number of undertakings that can be scored ranges from a high of 26 for Bonn I (1978) down to only 4 for Tokyo II (1986). The average scores differ greatly by summit, ranging from 0.8 or more for Versailles (1982) and Venice (1987) to low or negative readings for Williamsburg (1983) and Toronto (1988). These scores, which are intended to measure only the degree of compliance with specific summit undertakings in the area of macroeconomics and energy, may not correlate closely with the degree of "success" attributed to the summits by those who rate them on other grounds.

Former German Chancellor Schmidt (1985, p. 126), for instance, rates the first economic summit as "probably the best." With the press kept at a distance, he wrote, "we had to concentrate on our five partners," and we left Rambouillet "with the feeling that we were thus better able to cooperate with one another." Yet, the performance score shown for the undertakings of the 1975 summit (Table 4) is not far above the overall average. Putnam and Bayne (1987, p. 135) described Versailles as the first "failed" summit, because it left very bad feelings, but then added that "Versailles would prove to be a substantive success, though a procedural failure" (p. 140). They concluded that the next summit, Williamsburg, was a success when "measured against lowered expectations" (p. 181), yet we have given Williamsburg a very low compliance score. Indeed, unusually high scores at one summit, such as those for Tokyo I (1979), Versailles (1982), and Venice II (1987), tend to be followed by unusually low scores at the next, without, however, suggesting an entirely firm pattern. In addition, there appears to be no systematic relation at all between the number of undertakings that can be scored in a particular summit declaration and the level of the average scores for that summit.

Although summits have been rated informally by others, no one appears to have made summary ratings of the credibility of commitments by individual country. Yet the political circumstances of national governments may differ in ways that bear on their willingness and ability to deliver. If commitments are made at a summit primarily to strengthen a government's hand against political opposition in its own country—be it opposition from within the ruling coalition, other branches of government, or beyond—performance risk is high, for the commitments would not be supported by a prior national consensus. Hence, the national policy regime and performance on international commitments need not be independent (as Roubini and Sachs, 1989, and Eichengreen, 1992, have shown). All the same, because the strength and resolution of governments in several summit countries has clearly changed dramatically during the fifteen-year period considered, we shall not pursue such political theories or project them onto particular countries.

Unsupported Conjectures

It is interesting to note that common conjectures related, not to variables of domestic governance, but to (1) differences in international exposure, (2) problems in assigning responsibility for the production of public goods, or (3) the technical controllability of outcomes, receive no support from the pattern of scores in Table 5. For example:

Conjecture 1. Asymmetries in the degree to which countries can visit macroeconomic externalities upon each other depend largely on their economic size. These differences in exposure relate, in turn, to differences in the degree to which the S-7 countries can exert effective pressure on each other (see Dobson, 1991, p. 127). Because large countries are not nearly as concerned with the undertakings of small countries as small countries are with large, small countries attempt to gain leverage over large countries by scrupulously honoring their commitments. By setting a good example, they may hope to strengthen respect for international commitments generally. This is the opposite presumption from that made about small members of a cartel, who may be inclined to cheat because of their relative impunity. The reason for the difference is that, in the area of international macroeconomic policy coordination, small countries can reduce their vulnerability by boosting the international coordination process and its egalitarian elements. They invest in the process by strict adherence to commitments and by refusing to take advantage, through cheating, of their comparative lack of influence on the collective outcome.

Evidence. No systematic pattern of asymmetry by size of country is supported by the data. The smallest (by GDP) of the S-7 countries, Canada, has the second-highest score, after the United Kingdom, whereas the second smallest, Italy, has a low score. The two largest countries, the United States and Japan, have low scores, but not as low as France, which is much smaller. The evidence thus appears unkind to any theory linking the degree of performance simply to the size of the countries measured by GNP.

Conjecture 2. Multi-country undertakings, to which every country is to contribute, are likely to be honored less closely than single-country undertakings because diffusion of accountability creates free-rider problems. Unless assignments can be parceled out clearly, so that the contribution key is fixed, countries will not provide adequately for the

37

TABLE 5

AVERAGE, STANDARD DEVIATION, AND NUMBER OF SCORES FOR SUMMIT UNDERTAKINGS, 1975-1989

	Average	SD	N	$(N - 1)^{-0.5a}$
By Country, by Size of 1980 GNP				
United States	0.286	0.707	33	0.177
Japan	0.269	0.649	29	0.189
Germany	0.340	0.739	24	0.209
France	0.239	0.613	24	0.209
United Kingdom	0.411	0.757	21	0.224
Italy	0.281	0.680	27	0.196
Canada	0.391	0.662	26	0.200
All Undertakings	0.317	0.688	209	0.069
All Single-Country	0.313	0.689	184	0.074
All Multi-Country	0.349	0.681	25	0.204
By Function and Controllability				
Real GNP Growth	0.432	0.625	18	0.243
Demand Composition	0.268	0.825	7	0.408
International Trade	0.758	0.358	7	0.408
Fiscal Adjustments	0.263	0.692	40	0.160
Interest Rate	0.266	0.547	21	0.224
Inflation Rate	0.222	0.727	84	0.110
Foreign-Exchange Rate	−0.720	0.281	2	1.000
Aid and Schedules	0.265	0.388	5	0.500
Energy	0.668	0.558	25	0.204
All Direct Policy Measures	0.278	0.635	10	0.333
All Other Measures	0.319	0.691	199	0.071
All Except Energy	0.269	0.690	184	0.074
All Except Inflation	0.381	0.653	125	0.090

SOURCE: Unpublished appendix available from authors (see Chapter 3, note 5).

[a] Standard deviation (SD) of the average score under the joint null hypothesis that the population value of the SD of scores is 1 because summit ambition and effect are both 0.

production of public goods. Hence, collective undertakings that cannot easily be refracted into national obligations may receive less compliance than undertakings singling out particular nations.

Evidence. Average scores differ little between multi-country and single-country undertakings. Indeed, the average level of scores shown in Table 5 is (insignificantly) higher for commitments of the collective kind. Multi-country commitments have referred to achieving greater energy independence or higher economic growth for the S-7 countries as a group and to reducing current-account imbalances and exchange-rate volatility between them. They have also involved calls for the timely completion of international negotiations and agreements in which the S-7 are centrally involved. Even though the public-goods aspects of such multi-country undertakings are thus quite apparent, the degree of compliance has been no less than for commitments that could be assigned specifically to individual countries, such as commitments to reduce inflation and fiscal deficits.

Conjecture 3. Undertakings that specify the use of policy instruments are likely to be fulfilled to a greater degree than undertakings that are more dependent on economic processes and macroeconomic interactions with the private sector. As Putnam and Henning (1989, p. 102) have noted, participants in international coordination came to appreciate the superiority of agreements that specified policy moves, rather than economic outcomes, about a decade ago, presumably because they could manage the former more closely than the latter. Kenen (1989, p. 89) also advises governments "to frame their commitments in terms of their policy instruments, rather than the mixture of targets and instruments currently used by the G-7 governments."[1] Indeed, Kenen (1990, p. 66) regards "commitments about instruments" as "the distinguishing feature of coordination, setting it apart from other forms of economic cooperation."

Evidence. Table 5 shows a *lower* score for commitments involving direct policy measures than for all other undertakings. Hence, the data do not support the idea that commitments are more credible when limited to measures governments can control directly. Rather, governments appear to have at least as much difficulty adopting the policy measures promised as they have with forecasting other developments and their effects on target variables endogenous to the economic system. Nevertheless, the detail by function in Table 5 suggests that pledges about variables that are subject to a large variety of extrinsic shocks or to intrinsic instability may be otiose. Commitments to "greater exchange-rate stability," which receive a negative score, are a case in point. Yet, even those commitments relating to energy production and consumption that do not involve direct policy measures are subject to long-term policy influences. These may have made the outcome of such commitments relatively controllable.

In any event, the degree to which energy commitments have been fulfilled in the past stands out from commitments in all other areas. The figures in the last column of Table 5 represent the population values of

---

[1] Williamson and Miller (1987, p. 64) classify the 10 variables suggested at the 1986 Tokyo summit as suitable indicators for international surveillance: 4 are classified as targets, 2 as instruments, 1 as an intermediate target, and 3 as redundant.

the standard deviations of the average scores under the null hypothesis that the population values of those scores are 0. Using these values to test the significance levels of the average scores reported in the first column, we find that, of the nine functional areas distinguished, only commitments in the area of energy have received a positive score that is statistically significant at the 1-percent level. This might suggest that summit pledges are less reliable when they concern standard macroeconomic issues than when they concern reforms that are more microeconomic or "structural" in character, involving a sustained reordering of competitive conditions and production incentives.

The Low Level of Scores

As reported in Chapter 2, a number of researchers have agreed that "deals struck at the summit" are highly credible. Our results tend to contradict that expectation at least with regard to those deals embodied in economic declarations. Indeed, our most striking finding is the low average score for compliance with the 209 undertakings extracted from the first fifteen summit declarations. Contrary to the views of those representing summit undertakings as substantially honored, though perhaps ill advised, the combined score is only 0.32. The average score falls to 0.27 when the 25 distinct undertakings in the field of energy are omitted. It rises to 0.38 when the 84 undertakings to reduce inflation are excluded. Under our cardinal scoring methodology, the results support the conclusion that the macroeconomic undertakings have been only partly fulfilled, to a degree that is, on average, slightly less than one-third.

These values are all statistically significant at the 1-percent level, given that the number of undertakings, taken together, is large enough to produce a small standard deviation of the mean (less than 0.1). In other words, we can reject the joint hypothesis of "no summit ambition" and "no summit effect" when applied to the whole set of commitments. Nevertheless, the average scores are so low and their scatter so high that we must question whether the newsworthiness of the summits can rest mainly on the credibility of the commitments announced in the economic declarations. The standard deviations of the individual scores tend to be 0.6 or more in any group and close to 0.7 for the entire set of scores. Values in this range can be deemed to support the view that commitments contained in the summit declarations are shots taken in very poor light, if not entirely in the dark. Indeed, when mapped into the grid of experimental results laid out in Table 3, a mean of about 0.3 and a standard deviation of 0.7 are consistent with targeting a change equal to about one standard deviation from where we would otherwise expect the variable to be, and achieving considerably less on average. If the counterfactual economic data without "summit effect" are generated by a random walk, and, if summit commitments are meant to bring policy influences to bear on the next step, then the declarations are credible in moving these data somewhat in the desired direction, but only barely.[2]

Why are the scores so low? The explanation may perhaps be found in the discussion in Chapter 4 concerning the reasons why specific issues become the subjects of summit commitments. If heads of state need to be seen as actively confronting the problems most troubling to their voting public, they cannot readily avoid public promises to deal with those problems. If their constituents are acutely conscious of a turn for the worse or of a problem that has continued to fester, it is difficult not to respond to the common expectation that "something should be done" at the grand occasion provided by the summit. The principals will therefore attempt to satisfy such expectations by publicly offering remedial action or an improved outlook even if the hope for success is low, but not so low that dismal failure is practically inevitable. It may be safer for politicians to address macroeconomic distress in their declarations, even with a risk of failing, than to be seen as not being able or caring enough to try at all.

---

[2] If the average score were low, say 0.3, but the standard deviation of scores were equally low, say 0.1, then the public would learn to take each grain of commitment with a little over two grains of salt. Dividing any change promised by 10/3 could then come close to netting out the true commitments underlying any particular announcement. Hence, any announcements made with a known and steady degree of exaggeration could be credible even if the average degree of compliance is predictably small. In fact, however, the dispersion of the individual scores was found to be generally much larger than their mean, so that little understanding would be gained by "deflating" all commitments uniformly by their average degree of compliance.

7   CONCLUDING COMMENTS

Much in this study deals with words in a new way that can be relevant to an analysis of international compacts in other fields. Most important obligations between nations, such as peace treaties or treaties of mutual assistance or cooperation, are couched principally in words rather than numbers. Invariably, the undertakings or goals agreed to are vague in at least some respects, but this does not make them unimportant or unsuitable for verification through methodical work.

To express vagueness in a calculable way, we have used membership functions to define the content of these goals and of the obligations they have imposed, thereby allowing deviations to be scored in terms of relative success or failure. Clearly, we cannot have avoided subjective judgment altogether in identifying the substance of an undertaking and couching it in a form suitable for continuous scoring. We have also made choices about the mathematical scoring functions and about the intervals over which they should be fitted. As in any assessment of compliance or achievement, however, confidence in the fairness and consistency of a chosen procedure may be enhanced by knowing, first, what it is and, second, how it is applied.

Despite a residual subjective element in our "best judgment," we doubt that any other group of researchers would rate the overall record of compliance very differently if their scoring were disciplined by the same basic approach. That approach starts with an interpretation of the text of the economic declarations, and not with prejudgments or impressions gained elsewhere. It then audits the commitments in order to provide information on what deserve to be called the stylized facts about the degree of compliance. Establishing that degree empirically is important in assessing the quality of the commitment. If there is only low compliance with the economic declaration, which is the centerpiece of the summit and one of the most prominent public documents through which international coordination can work and accountability be established, the declaration cannot be considered credible or very important regardless of what one may think about the wisdom of its prescriptions or predictions.

Public perceptions are important, but so are the facts that ultimately form them. A recent study of international opinion surveys (Wertman and Smith, 1989) found that a clear majority of those interviewed in

42

S-7 countries other than the United States considered it very, or at least fairly, important to coordinate policies closely with the United States. United States commentators do not necessarily reciprocate the sentiment. Feldstein (1988, p. 9), for instance, has advised that "the process of international cooperation in macroeconomic and exchange rate management" be shut down because it can be harmful. Others, such as Brady (1990), have been much more positive. Obviously, opinions about the usefulness of summits differ greatly, although it is not clear on what evidence such views turn.

When heads of government confer, there is no such thing as "just talk," although there are undoubtedly stretches of idleness and wasted motion to be traversed.[1] Like talk, fuzzy declarations can be full of meaning and implications. The wording of declarations, unlike conversations, is most carefully considered. Indeed, even if the goals congealed in the writs of the summit could be made entirely crisp, the concrete obligations and means of implementation would still need to remain fuzzy in at least some respects. Sovereigns may plan a joint campaign, but they do not accept strict marching orders or meticulous commandments from each other, even when some are obviously more powerful than others.

Fuzziness and credibility are both essential to agreement under these conditions. Indeed, the greater the credibility of the basic intentions, the fuzzier an announcement can be without depriving it of informational content (see Cukierman and Meltzer, 1986). The importance of trust can, in turn, be increased by not trying to be overly precise, means-specific, or exhaustive. Indeed, the choice of generality directs attention to the overall spirit of an undertaking and to the culture of coordination in which it arose.

The summit process is an important part and symbol of this culture of coordination. At the same time, the fact that undertakings remain largely unfulfilled means that the process has as yet acquired little binding force and that fuzziness and credibility have not been supporting each other in this regard. Rather, the low level of credibility may have made fuzziness indicative of a lack of commitment. If "effective institutions raise the benefits of cooperative solutions or the costs of defection" (North, 1991, p. 98), and the economic declarations are the main institutional product of the summit process, the product has yet to prove itself as deserving of much credit with the public.

---

[1] Malkin's (1987, pp. 258-261) deadly, almost first-hand account of the supine proceedings at the 1982 Versailles summit makes this depressingly clear.

This skeptical conclusion is the result of a large amount of empirical work with both words and numbers, not the consequence of a quick helping of economic ideology or game-theoretic hypotheses. We hope that our work will stimulate interest in future studies to determine not just what international coordination *can* do, but what it *has* done, by what means, and why it may have done much less than its proponents have believed.

APPENDIX: MEAN AND STANDARD DEVIATION OF SCORES EXPECTED UNDER DIFFERENT CONDITIONS

This Appendix explains how the hypothetical sample means and standard deviations of scores shown in Table 3 of Chapter 5 are calculated under various conditions. Because the statistical specifications and the procedure for deriving population values are quite general, the work may of interest beyond its immediate area of application.

The cases selected to establish a grid of reference values are identified in Table A-1 below. They are distinguished by the strength of the undertaking targeted and the effect actually achieved. In the three cases along the principal diagonal, the strength of the actual effect is as large as targeted, but in all other cases it is less. Effects targeted and achieved are represented by reductions in some "bad," such as inflation, measured in multiples of their step-ahead standard deviations, σ_u. Except in cases 1.1, 1.2, and 1.3, where the summit effect (c) is 0 and the status quo undisturbed, the normal distribution of stochastic outcomes is assumed to shift to the left from the status quo, as shown in the three lower diagrams in Figure A-1. Scores fall linearly from 1 for fully (or more than fully) achieving the change targeted to 0 for simply repeating the status quo. They are extended symmetrically to the negative range for even worse outcomes. The deviations in the inflation outcomes from their values expected with summit effect, in step-ahead normal deviates or standard units, $z = (x_t - x_{t-1} - c)/\sigma_u$, are shown along the horizontal axes of the case diagrams. The scores corresponding to the outcomes, whose relative frequency is indicated by the bell-shaped curves, are shown on the vertical axes. These axes are always drawn at the level representing the status quo so that the expected value of the new outcomes lies to the left of the vertical axes in all cases in which there is a summit effect $(c < 0)$. Reference to the diagrams is helpful in deriving the mean and standard deviation of the scores expected in each of the six cases.

Derivation of the Population Values of the Average Scores

Cases 1.1 to 1.3. As can easily be seen from the corresponding figures, the population mean of scores, A, is 0 as long as there is no summit effect $(c = 0)$.

45

TABLE A-1

OVERVIEW OF CASES CONSIDERED

			Summit Ambition	
		$X_t - x_{t-1} = 0$	$X_t - x_{t-1} = -\sigma_u$	$X_t - x_{t-1} = -2\sigma_u$
	0	1.1	1.2	1.3
Summit Effect (c)	$-\sigma_u$		2.2	2.3
	$-2\sigma_u$			3.3

NOTE: Table 3 reports results calculated for these six cases.

Case 2.2. If there is a summit effect equal to $-\sigma_u$, 50 percent of the outcomes receive a score of 1 for, say, desirable reductions of inflation at least as large as σ_u. There is no penalty for doing more than promised. Another 2.27 percent receive a score of -1 for increases in inflation in excess of σ_u from its current level (and, therefore, in excess of $2\sigma_u$ from the reduced level promised). In between, scores (s) fall from $+1$ when the normal deviate (z) is 0, to -1 when the normal deviate, from the mean of the distribution that was shifted to the left by 1 through the summit effect, is 2.

These two matching pairs of values for s and z will be used to translate s into z. To find the expected value of s when s is distributed according to the frequency function for the normal deviate z, we must first obtain the parameters of the line segment connecting all intermediate values of s to values of z. The form of this line segment is $s = a + bz$. Substituting the pairs of (s, z) values identified above into this linear scoring function yields $a = +1$ and $b = -1$. Hence s can be replaced by $a + bz = 1 - z$ in the intermediate range leading from $s = -1$ $(z = 2)$ to $s = 1$ $(z = 0)$. The contribution of this range to the value of the population mean is:

$$\int_0^2 \frac{1}{\sqrt{2\pi}} e^{-\frac{z^2}{2}} (1 - z)dz = \int_0^2 \frac{1}{\sqrt{2\pi}} e^{-\frac{z^2}{2}} dz + \frac{1}{\sqrt{2\pi}} e^{-\frac{z^2}{2}} \Big|_0^2$$

$$= 0.4773 + 0.0540 - 0.3989$$

$$= 0.1324.$$

The value of the population mean is $0.50 - 0.0227 + 0.1324 = 0.6097$.

46

Case 2.3. Here, the undertaking is twice as ambitious as the summit effect of σ_u actually achieved. Now, only 15.87 percent of the outcomes are expected to receive a score of 1. But the ambitious undertaking distends the intermediate scoring range, given that repeating the current level of inflation is always scored 0. Therefore, only 0.13 percent of the outcomes receive a score of −1. In the intermediate range, the score is +1 for $z = -1$, and −1 for $z = 3$, so that $a = 0.5$, $b = -0.5$,

FIGURE A-1

THE DISTRIBUTION OF OUTCOMES, COMPARED WITH THE STATUS QUO, AND THE
SCORES ASSOCIATED WITH THEM IN SIX CASES

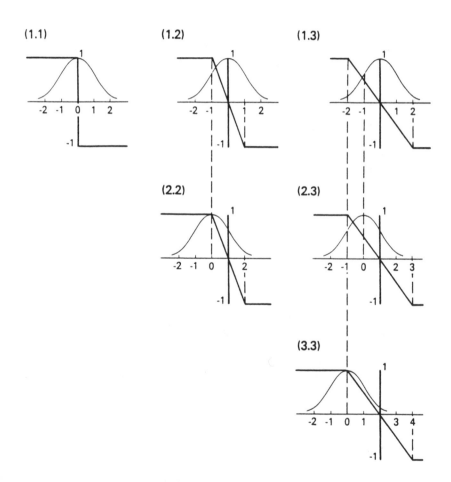

and $s = 0.5(1 - z)$. The contribution of the intermediate range to the value of the population mean is:

$$\int_{-1}^{3} \frac{0.5}{\sqrt{2\pi}} e^{-\frac{z^2}{2}} (1 - z)\,dz = 0.3012.$$

The value of the population mean is $0.1587 - 0.0013 + 0.3012 = 0.4586$.

Case 3.3. Here, the summit effect is again as large as the undertaking, but both are $-2\sigma_u$. Hence, 50 percent of the expected outcomes receive a score of 1, and practically none receives a score of -1 in a range that is 4 or more normal deviates away. In the intermediate range, the score is $+1$ for $z = 0$, and -1 for $z = 4$, so that $a = 1$, $b = -0.5$, and $s = 1 - 0.5z$. The contribution of the intermediate range to the value of the population mean is:

$$\int_{0}^{4} \frac{1}{\sqrt{2\pi}} e^{-\frac{z^2}{2}} (1 - 0.5z)\,dz = 0.3006.$$

The value of the population mean is $0.50 + 0.3006 = 0.8006$.

Derivation of the Population Values of the Standard Deviations of Scores

Case 1.1. Because scores must be either $+1$ or -1 with equal probability in this case of no ambition, the squared differences from the mean of 0 are 1 for each of the N observations. Hence the variance and the standard deviation, SD, of the scores are $N/N = 1$.

Case 1.2. The contribution to the variance of the scores that comes from the extremes, $+1$ and -1, is 0.3174, the area under the normal curve beyond the deviates -1 and $+1$. Between these extremes, the score, s, equals $-z$, so that $s^2 = z^2$. Hence, the contribution to the variance of scores is:

$$\int_{-1}^{1} \frac{1}{\sqrt{2\pi}} e^{-\frac{z^2}{2}} z^2\,dz.$$

48

Integrating by parts, let:

$$v = \int_{-1}^{1} \frac{z}{\sqrt{2\pi}} e^{-\frac{z^2}{2}} dz = -\frac{1}{\sqrt{2\pi}} e^{-\frac{z^2}{2}} \Big|_{-1}^{1}, \text{ and } u = z.$$

Then $\int uv' = uv - \int u'v$ corresponds to:

$$\int_{-1}^{1} \left(\frac{1}{\sqrt{2\pi}} e^{-\frac{z^2}{2}} z \right) z\, dz = -\frac{z}{\sqrt{2\pi}} e^{-\frac{z^2}{2}} \Big|_{-1}^{1} + 2\int_{0}^{1} \frac{1}{\sqrt{2\pi}} e^{-\frac{z^2}{2}} dz$$

$$= -0.4839 + 0.6826$$

$$= 0.1987.$$

The population variance of the score is 0.3174 + 0.1987 = 0.5161, and the standard deviation, SD, is 0.7184.

Case 1.3. The contribution to the variance of the score that comes from the extremes of +1 and −1 is now reduced to 0.0454, the area beyond the normal deviates −2 and +2. Between the extremes, the score, s, is $-0.5z$, or $s^2 = 0.25z^2$. Hence, the contribution to the variance of scores is:

$$\int_{-2}^{2} \frac{1}{4\sqrt{2\pi}} e^{-\frac{z^2}{2}} z^2 dz = 0.1847.$$

The population variance of the score is 0.0454 + 0.1847 = 0.2301, so SD is 0.4797.

Case 2.2. The calculation of the population variance of the scores becomes more difficult when there is a summit effect, so that the population mean (A) ceases to be zero. Subtracting the population mean of 0.6097 from the extreme scores of −1 and +1, respectively, makes their combined contribution to the variance $0.50(1 - 0.6097)^2 + 0.0227(-1 - 0.6097)^2 = 0.1350$. Furthermore, in the intermediate range,

49

where $s = 1 - z$, $s - A = 0.3903 - z$, so that $(s - A)^2 = 0.1523 - 0.7806z + z^2$. Hence, the contribution to the variance of score is:

$$\int_0^2 \frac{1}{\sqrt{2\pi}} e^{-\frac{z^2}{2}} (0.1523 - 0.7806z + z^2) dz = 0.1728.$$

The population variance is $0.1350 + 0.1728 = 0.3078$, so SD is 0.5548.

Case 2.3. The mean previously derived for this case was 0.4586. Given that $s = 0.5(1 - z)$, $(s - A)^2 = 0.25(0.0828 - z)^2 = 0.0017 - 0.0414z + 0.25z^2$. Subtracting the mean from the 15.87 percent of cases receiving a score of +1 and from the 0.13 percent receiving a score of −1 yields the contribution to the population variance coming from the extremes. It is $0.1587(1 - 0.4586)^2 + 0.0013(-1 - 0.4586)^2 = 0.0493$. The contribution of scores in the intermediate range is:

$$\int_{-1}^3 \frac{1}{\sqrt{2\pi}} e^{-\frac{z^2}{2}} (0.0017 - 0.0414z + 0.25z^2) dz = 0.1378.$$

The population variance is $0.0493 + 0.1378 = 0.1871$, so SD is 0.4326.

Case 3.3. The value of the population mean is 0.8006, so that the extreme scores contribute an amount equal to $0.5000(1 - 0.8006)^2 + 0.0000(-1 - 0.8006)^2 = 0.0199$. Furthermore, $s = 1 - 0.5z$ and $(s - A) = 0.1994 - 0.5z$, so that $(s - A)^2 = 0.0398 - 0.1994z + 0.25z^2$. The contribution of scores in the intermediate range is:

$$\int_0^4 \frac{1}{\sqrt{2\pi}} e^{-\frac{z^2}{2}} (0.0398 - 0.1994z + 0.25z^2) dz = 0.0653.$$

The population variance is $0.0199 + 0.0653 = 0.0852$, so SD is 0.2919.

REFERENCES

Alesina, Alberto, Alessandro Prati, and Guido Tabellini, "Public Confidence and Debt Management: A Model and a Case Study for Italy," in Rudiger Dornbusch and Mario Draghi, eds., *Public Debt Management: Theory and History*, Cambridge and New York, Cambridge University Press, 1990, pp. 94-118.

Atlantic Council of the United States, Working Group on Political Affairs, *Summit Meetings and Collective Leadership in the 1980's*, Washington, D.C., The Atlantic Council, April 1980.

Bergsten, Fred, "A New Big Three to Manage the World Economy," *Challenge*, 33 (November-December 1990), pp. 17-25.

Bini Smaghi, Lorenzo, "Exchange Rate Variability and Trade: Why is it so Difficult to Find Any Empirical Relationship?" *Banca d'Italia Temi di Discussione*, No. 145, December 1990.

Blackburn, Keith, and Michael Christensen, "Monetary Policy and Policy Credibility," *Journal of Economic Literature*, 27 (March 1989), pp. 1-45.

Brady, Nicholas F., "Remarks by The Honorable Nicholas F. Brady, Secretary of the Treasury, before the American Chamber of Commerce (United Kingdom), London, May 29," *Treasury News*, 1990, NB-825.

Branson, William H., "Comment," in William H. Branson, Jacob A. Frenkel, and Morris Goldstein, eds., *International Policy Coordination and Exchange Rate Fluctuations*, Chicago, University of Chicago Press, 1990, pp. 59-62.

Canzoneri, Matthew B., and Dale W. Henderson, *Monetary Policy in Interdependent Economies: A Game-Theoretic Approach*, Cambridge, Mass., MIT Press, 1991.

Chouraqui, Jean-Claude, Robert P. Hagemann, and Nicola Sartor, "Indicators of Fiscal Policy: A Reassessment," OECD Department of Economics and Statistics Working Paper No. 78, Paris, Organisation of Economic Cooperation and Development, April 1990.

Cukierman, Alex, and Allan H. Meltzer, "The Credibility of Monetary Announcements," in Manfred J. M. Neumann, ed., *Monetary Policy and Uncertainty: Collected Papers from the 1982-1984 Konstanz Seminars*, Baden-Baden, Nomos Verlagsgesellschaft, 1986, pp. 39-67.

Currie, David A., Gerald Holtham, and A. Hughes Hallett, "The Theory and Practice of International Policy Coordination: Does Coordination Pay?" in Ralph C. Bryant, David A. Currie, Jacob A. Frenkel, Paul R. Masson, and Richard Portes, eds., *Macroeconomic Policies in an Interdependent World*, Washington, D.C., International Monetary Fund, 1989, pp. 14-46.

Dobson, Wendy, *Economic Policy Coordination: Requiem or Prologue?*, Washington, D.C., Institute for International Economics, 1991.

Dornbusch, Rudiger, "Policy and Performance Links between LDC Debtors and Industrial Nations," *Brookings Papers on Economic Activity*, No. 2 (1985), pp. 303-356.

———, "Exchange Rate Economics: 1986," *The Economic Journal*, 97 (March 1987), pp. 1-18.

Eichengreen, Barry, "Hegemonic Stability Theories of the International Monetary System," in Richard N. Cooper, Barry Eichengreen, Gerald Holtham, Robert D. Putnam, and C. Randall Henning, eds., *Can Nations Agree?: Issues in International Economic Cooperation*, Washington, D.C., The Brookings Institution, 1989, pp. 255-298.

———, *Gold Fetters: Gold Standard and Depressions*, New York, Oxford University Press, 1992.

European Communities, Directorate General for Economic and Financial Affairs, *European Economy: Annual Review*, No. 7 (November 1980).

Feldstein, Martin, "International Economic Cooperation: Introduction," in Martin Feldstein, ed., *International Economic Cooperation*, Chicago, University of Chicago Press, 1988, pp. 1-10.

Fischer, Stanley, "International Macroeconomic Policy Coordination," in Martin Feldstein, ed., *International Economic Cooperation*, Chicago, University of Chicago Press, 1988, pp. 1-43.

Frankel, Jeffrey A., "Obstacles to Coordination and a Consideration of Two Proposals to Overcome Them: International Nominal Targeting (INT) and the Hosomi Fund," in William H. Branson, Jacob A. Frenkel, and Morris Goldstein, eds., *International Policy Coordination and Exchange Rate Fluctuations*, Chicago, University of Chicago Press, 1990, pp. 109-145.

Frenkel, Jacob A., Morris Goldstein, and Paul R. Masson, "International Coordination of Economic Policies: Scope, Methods, and Effects," in Wilfried Guth, moderator, *Economic Policy Coordination*, Washington, D.C., International Monetary Fund, 1988, pp. 149-192.

Frenkel, Jacob A., and Assaf Razin, "The Mundell-Fleming Model a Quarter Century Later: A Unified Exposition," *International Monetary Fund Staff Papers*, 34 (No. 4, December 1987), pp. 567-620.

Funabashi, Yoichi, *Managing the Dollar: From the Plaza to the Louvre*, Washington, D.C., Institute for International Economics, 1988 (2nd ed., rev., 1989).

Ghosh, Atish R., and Paul R. Masson, "Model Uncertainty, Learning, and the Gains from Coordination," *The American Economic Review*, 81 (June 1991), pp. 465-479.

Hajnal, Peter I., *The Seven-Power Summit: Documents from the Summits of the Industrialized Countries, 1975-1989*, Millwood, N.Y., Kraus International, 1989.

Helliwell, John F., "The Fiscal Deficit and the External Deficit: Siblings but not Twins," in Rudolph G. Penner, ed., *The Great Fiscal Experiment*, Washington, D.C., The Urban Institute, 1991, pp. 23-58.

Herz, Bernhard, and Joachim Starbatty, "Zur Frage internationaler Dominanz-beziehungen—-eine Analyse der Machtverteilung auf Weltwirtschaftsgipfe-ln," Tuebingen, Department of Economics, University of Tuebingen, June 1990, processed.

Holtham, Gerald, "German Macroeconomic Policy and the 1978 Bonn Summit," in Richard N. Cooper, Barry Eichengreen, Gerald Holtham, Robert D. Putnam, and C. Randall Henning, eds., *Can Nations Agree?: Issues in International Economic Cooperation*, Washington, D.C., The Brookings Institution, 1989, pp. 144-177.

Hooper, Peter, and Catherine L. Mann, *The Emergence and Persistence of the U.S. External Imbalance, 1980-87*, Princeton Studies in International Finance No. 65, Princeton, N.J., Princeton University, International Finance Section, October 1989.

Hoskins, W. Lee, "International Policy Coordination: Can We Afford It?" *Economic Commentary*, Federal Reserve Bank of Cleveland, January 1, 1989.

Hughes Hallett, Andrew J., "International Policy Design and the Sustainability of Policy Bargains," *Journal of Economic Dynamics and Control*, 10 December 1986), pp. 467-494.

————, "How Robust are the Gains to Policy Coordination to Variations in the Model and Objectives?" *Ricerche Economiche*, 41 (November-December 1987), pp. 341-372.

Hughes Hallett, Andrew J., Gerald Holtham, and Gary Hutson, "Exchange-Rate Targetting as Surrogate International Cooperation," in Marcus Miller, Barry Eichengreen, and Richard Portes, eds., *Blueprints for Exchange-Rate Management*, London, Academic Press, 1989, pp. 239-278.

Humpage, Owen F., "A Hitchhiker's Guide to International Macroeconomic Policy Coordination," Federal Reserve Bank of Cleveland *Economic Review*, 26 (1990:I), pp. 2-14.

International Monetary Fund (IMF), *International Financial Statistics*, various issues, Washington, D.C., International Monetary Fund, 1975-1991.

Kahler, Miles, "Organization and Cooperation: International Institutions and Policy Coordination," *Journal of Public Policy*, 8 (July-December 1988), pp. 375-401.

Kenen, Peter B., *Exchange Rates and Policy Coordination*, Ann Arbor, University of Michigan Press, 1989.

————, "The Coordination of Macroeconomic Policies," in William H. Branson, Jacob A. Frenkel, and Morris Goldstein, eds., *International Policy Coordination and Exchange Rate Fluctuations*, Chicago, University of Chicago Press, 1990, pp. 63-102.

Keohane, Robert O., *After Hegemony: Cooperation and Discord in the World Political Economy*, Princeton, N.J., Princeton University Press, 1984.

Krasner, Stephen D., "Structural Causes and Regime Consequences: Regimes as Intervening Variables," *International Organization*, 36 (Spring 1982), pp. 185-205.

Krugman, Paul R., "International Adjustment 1985-90: What Have We Learned?" *International Economic Insights*, 1 (November/December 1990), pp. 20-21.

Krugman, Paul R., and Richard E. Baldwin, "The Persistence of the U.S. Trade Deficit," *Brookings Papers on Economic Activity*, No. 1 (1987), pp. 1-43.

Malkin, Lawrence, *The National Debt*, New York, Henry Holt, 1987.

Marris, Stephen N., *Deficits and the Dollar: The World Economy at Risk*, Washington, D.C., Institute for International Economics, 1985 (rev. ed., 1987).

Minford, Patrick, "Exchange-Rate Regimes and Policy Coordination," in Marcus Miller, Barry Eichengreen, and Richard Portes, eds., *Blueprints for Exchange-Rate Management*, London, Academic Press, 1989, pp. 207-235.

North, Douglass C., "Institutions," *The Journal of Economic Perspectives*, 5 (Winter 1991), pp. 97-112.

Obstfeld, Maurice, "The Effectiveness of Foreign-Exchange Intervention: Recent Experience, 1985-1988," in William H. Branson, Jacob A. Frenkel, and Morris Goldstein, eds., *International Policy Coordination and Exchange Rate Fluctuations*, Chicago, University of Chicago Press, 1990, pp. 197-237.

Organisation for Economic Co-Operation and Development, *OECD Economic Outlook*, No. 33 (July 1983).

———, *OECD Economic Outlook*, No. 46 (December 1989).

———, *OECD Economic Outlook*, No. 48 (December 1990).

Ostry, Sylvia, "Canada, Europe and the Economic Summits," The Hague, All-European Canadian Studies Conference, October 24-27, 1990, processed.

Oudiz, Gilles, and Jeffrey Sachs, "Macroeconomic Policy Coordination Among the Industrial Economies," *Brookings Papers on Economic Activity*, No. 1, 1984, pp. 175.

———, "International Policy Coordination in Dynamic Macroeconomic Models," in Willem H. Buiter and Richard C. Marston, eds., *International Economic Policy Coordination*, Cambridge, Cambridge University Press, 1985, pp. 274-326.

Putnam, Robert D., and Nicholas Bayne, *Hanging Together: Cooperation and Conflict in the Seven-Power Summits*, Cambridge, Mass., Harvard University Press, 1987.

Putnam, Robert D., and C. Randall Henning, "The Bonn Summit of 1978: A Case Study in Coordination," in Richard N. Cooper, Barry Eichengreen, Gerald Holtham, Robert D. Putnam, and C. Randall Henning, eds., *Can Nations Agree?: Issues in International Economic Cooperation*, Washington, D.C., The Brookings Institution, 1989, pp. 12-140.

Rogoff, Kenneth S., "Can International Monetary Policy be Counterproductive?" *Journal of International Economics*, 18 (May 1985), pp. 199-217.

Roubini, Nouriel, and Jeffrey Sachs, "Government Spending and Budget Deficits in the Industrial Countries," *Economic Policy*, 8 (April 1989), pp. 100-132.

Ruggie, John G., "International Regimes, Transactions, and Change: Embedded Liberalism in the Postwar Economic Order," *International Organization*, 36 (Spring 1982), pp. 379-415.

Sachs, Jeffrey, and Charles Wyplosz, "La Politique Budgétaire et le Taux de Change Réel," *Annales de L'INSEE*, 53 (January-March 1984), pp. 63-92.

Schmidt, Helmut, *A Grand Strategy for the West: The Anachronism of National Strategies in an Interdependent World*, New Haven, Yale University Press, 1985.

Solomon, Robert, "Background Paper," in *Partners in Prosperity: The Report of the Twentieth Century Fund Task Force on the International Coordination of National Economic Policies*, New York, Priority Press, 1991, pp. 45-128.

Stein, Arthur A., "Coordination and Collaboration: Regimes in an Anarchic World," *International Organization*, 36 (Spring 1982), pp. 299-324.

Tanzi, Vito, and Mark S. Lutz, "Interest Rates and Government Debt: Are the Linkages Global Rather than National?" Paper prepared for the Symposium on The Political Economy of Government Debt held at De Nederlandsche Bank N.V., Amsterdam, June 21-24, 1990, Washington, D.C., International Monetary Fund, 1990, processed.

Taylor, John B., "International Coordination in the Design of Macroeconomic Policy Rules," *European Economic Review*, 28 (June-July 1985), pp. 53-81.

U.S. Department of Energy, Energy Information Administration, *1986 International Energy Annual*, Washington, D.C., Government Printing Office, 1987.

U.S. President, *Economic Report of the President*, Washington, D.C., Government Printing Office, February 1991.

Vaubel, Roland, "International Collusion or Competition for Macroeconomic Policy Coordination? A Restatement," *Recherches Économiques de Louvain*, 51 (December 1985), pp. 223-240.

von Furstenberg, George M., "Scoring the Success of Sanctions: A Review Article," *Open Economies Review*, 2 (No. 3, 1991), pp. 305-313.

———, ed., *Acting Under Uncertainty: Multidisciplinary Conceptions*, Boston, Kluwer, 1990.

von Furstenberg, George M., and Joseph P. Daniels, "Policy Undertakings by the Seven 'Summit' Countries: Ascertaining the Degree of Compliance," in Allan H. Meltzer and Charles I. Plosser, eds., *Carnegie-Rochester Conference Series on Public Policy*, 35 (Autumn 1991), pp. 267-308.

Wertman, Douglas A., and Steven K. Smith, "Summing Up Before the Economic Summit," *Public Opinion*, 11 (March/April 1989), pp. 41-45.

Williamson, John, and Marcus H. Miller, *Targets and Indicators: A Blueprint for the International Coordination of Economic Policy*, Washington, D.C., Institute for International Economics, 1987.

Zimmermann, H-J., *Fuzzy Set Theory and its Applications*, Boston, Kluwer, 1991.

PUBLICATIONS OF THE
INTERNATIONAL FINANCE SECTION

Notice to Contributors

The International Finance Section publishes papers in four series: ESSAYS IN INTERNATIONAL FINANCE, PRINCETON STUDIES IN INTERNATIONAL FINANCE, and SPECIAL PAPERS IN INTERNATIONAL ECONOMICS contain new work not published elsewhere. REPRINTS IN INTERNATIONAL FINANCE reproduce journal articles previously published by Princeton faculty members associated with the Section. The Section welcomes the submission of manuscripts for publication under the following guidelines:

ESSAYS are meant to disseminate new views about international financial matters and should be accessible to well-informed nonspecialists as well as to professional economists. Technical terms, tables, and charts should be used sparingly; mathematics should be avoided.

STUDIES are devoted to new research on international finance, with preference given to empirical work. They should be comparable in originality and technical proficiency to papers published in leading economic journals. They should be of medium length, longer than a journal article but shorter than a book.

SPECIAL PAPERS are surveys of research on particular topics and should be suitable for use in undergraduate courses. They may be concerned with international trade as well as international finance. They should also be of medium length.

Manuscripts should be submitted in triplicate, typed single sided and double spaced throughout on 8½ by 11 white bond paper. Publication can be expedited if manuscripts are computer keyboarded in WordPerfect 5.1 or a compatible program. Additional instructions and a style guide are available from the Section.

How to Obtain Publications

The Section's publications are distributed free of charge to college, university, and public libraries and to nongovernmental, nonprofit research institutions. Eligible institutions may ask to be placed on the Section's permanent mailing list.

Individuals and institutions not qualifying for free distribution may receive all publications for the calendar year for a subscription fee of $30.00. Late subscribers will receive all back issues for the year during which they subscribe. Subscribers should notify the Section promptly of any change in address, giving the old address as well as the new.

Publications may be ordered individually, with payment made in advance. ESSAYS and REPRINTS cost $6.50 each; STUDIES and SPECIAL PAPERS cost $9.00. An additional $1.25 should be sent for postage and handling within the United States, Canada, and Mexico; $1.50 should be added for surface delivery outside the region.

All payments must be made in U.S. dollars. Subscription fees and charges for single issues will be waived for organizations and individuals in countries where foreign-exchange regulations prohibit dollar payments.

Please address all correspondence, submissions, and orders to:

International Finance Section
Department of Economics, Fisher Hall
Princeton University
Princeton, New Jersey 08544-1021

List of Recent Publications

A complete list of publications may be obtained from the International Finance Section.

ESSAYS IN INTERNATIONAL FINANCE

155. Stephen Marris, *Managing the World Economy: Will We Ever Learn?* (October 1984)
156. Sebastian Edwards, *The Order of Liberalization of the External Sector in Developing Countries*. (December 1984)
157. Wilfred J. Ethier and Richard C. Marston, eds., with Kindleberger, Guttentag and Herring, Wallich, Henderson, and Hinshaw, *International Financial Markets and Capital Movements: A Symposium in Honor of Arthur I. Bloomfield*. (September 1985)
158. Charles E. Dumas, *The Effects of Government Deficits: A Comparative Analysis of Crowding Out*. (October 1985)
159. Jeffrey A. Frankel, *Six Possible Meanings of "Overvaluation": The 1981-85 Dollar*. (December 1985)
160. Stanley W. Black, *Learning from Adversity: Policy Responses to Two Oil Shocks*. (December 1985)
161. Alexis Rieffel, *The Role of the Paris Club in Managing Debt Problems*. (December 1985)
162. Stephen E. Haynes, Michael M. Hutchison, and Raymond F. Mikesell, *Japanese Financial Policies and the U.S. Trade Deficit*. (April 1986)
163. Arminio Fraga, *German Reparations and Brazilian Debt: A Comparative Study*. (July 1986)
164. Jack M. Guttentag and Richard J. Herring, *Disaster Myopia in International Banking*. (September 1986)
165. Rudiger Dornbusch, *Inflation, Exchange Rates, and Stabilization*. (October 1986)
166. John Spraos, *IMF Conditionality: Ineffectual, Inefficient, Mistargeted*. (December 1986)
167. Rainer Stefano Masera, *An Increasing Role for the ECU: A Character in Search of a Script*. (June 1987)
168. Paul Mosley, *Conditionality as Bargaining Process: Structural-Adjustment Lending, 1980-86*. (October 1987)

*Publications marked by an asterisk are out of print. They are available on demand in xerographic paperback or library-bound copies from University Microfilms International, Box 1467, Ann Arbor, Michigan 48106, USA, or 30-32 Mortimer St., London, WIN 7RA, England. Microfilm of all Essays by year is available from University Microfilms. Photocopied sheets of out-of-print titles are available from the Section at $9.00 per Essay and $11.00 per Study or Special Paper, plus $1.25 for domestic ($1.50 for overseas) postage and handling.

169. Paul Volcker, Ralph Bryant, Leonhard Gleske, Gottfried Haberler, Alexandre Lamfalussy, Shijuro Ogata, Jesús Silva-Herzog, Ross Starr, James Tobin, and Robert Triffin, *International Monetary Cooperation: Essays in Honor of Henry C. Wallich*. (December 1987)

170. Shafiqul Islam, *The Dollar and the Policy-Performance-Confidence Mix*. (July 1988)

171. James M. Boughton, *The Monetary Approach to Exchange Rates: What Now Remains?* (October 1988)

172. Jack M. Guttentag and Richard M. Herring, *Accounting for Losses On Sovereign Debt: Implications for New Lending*. (May 1989)

173. Benjamin J. Cohen, *Developing-Country Debt: A Middle Way*. (May 1989)

174. Jeffrey D. Sachs, *New Approaches to the Latin American Debt Crisis*. (July 1989)

175. C. David Finch, *The IMF: The Record and the Prospect*. (September 1989)

176. Graham Bird, *Loan-loss Provisions and Third-World Debt*. (November 1989)

177. Ronald Findlay, *The "Triangular Trade" and the Atlantic Economy of the Eighteenth Century: A Simple General-Equilibrium Model*. (March 1990)

178. Alberto Giovannini, *The Transition to European Monetary Union*. (November 1990)

179. Michael L. Mussa, *Exchange Rates in Theory and in Reality*. (December 1990)

180. Warren L. Coats, Jr., Reinhard W. Furstenberg, and Peter Isard, *The SDR System and the Issue of Resource Transfers*. (December 1990)

181. George S. Tavlas, *On the International Use of Currencies: The Case of the Deutsche Mark*. (March 1991)

182. Tommaso Padoa-Schioppa, ed., with Michael Emerson, Kumiharu Shigehara, and Richard Portes, *Europe after 1992: Three Essays*. (May 1991)

183. Michael Bruno, *High Inflation and the Nominal Anchors of an Open Economy*. (June 1991)

184. Jacques J. Polak, *The Changing Nature of IMF Conditionality*. (September 1991)

185. Ethan B. Kapstein, *Supervising International Banks: Origins and Implications of the Basle Accord*. (December 1991)

PRINCETON STUDIES IN INTERNATIONAL FINANCE

*54. Jeffrey Sachs, *Theoretical Issues in International Borrowing*. (July 1984)

55. Marsha R. Shelburn, *Rules for Regulating Intervention under a Managed Float*. (December 1984)

56. Paul De Grauwe, Marc Janssens and Hilde Leliaert, *Real-Exchange-Rate Variability from 1920 to 1926 and 1973 to 1982*. (September 1985)

57. Stephen S. Golub, *The Current-Account Balance and the Dollar: 1977-78 and 1983-84*. (October 1986)

58. John T. Cuddington, *Capital Flight: Estimates, Issues, and Explanations*. (December 1986)

59. Vincent P. Crawford, *International Lending, Long-Term Credit Relationships, and Dynamic Contract Theory*. (March 1987)

60. Thorvaldur Gylfason, *Credit Policy and Economic Activity in Developing Countries with IMF Stabilization Programs*. (August 1987)

61. Stephen A. Schuker, *American "Reparations" to Germany, 1919-33: Implications for the Third-World Debt Crisis*. (July 1988)
62. Steven B. Kamin, *Devaluation, External Balance, and Macroeconomic Performance: A Look at the Numbers*. (August 1988)
63. Jacob A. Frenkel and Assaf Razin, *Spending, Taxes, and Deficits: International-Intertemporal Approach*. (December 1988)
64. Jeffrey A. Frankel, *Obstacles to International Macroeconomic Policy Coordination*. (December 1988)
65. Peter Hooper and Catherine L. Mann, *The Emergence and Persistence of the U.S. External Imbalance, 1980-87*. (October 1989)
66. Helmut Reisen, *Public Debt, External Competitiveness, and Fiscal Discipline in Developing Countries*. (November 1989)
67. Victor Argy, Warwick McKibbin, and Eric Siegloff, *Exchange-Rate Regimes for a Small Economy in a Multi-Country World*. (December 1989)
68. Mark Gersovitz and Christina H. Paxson, *The Economies of Africa and the Prices of Their Exports*. (October 1990)
69. Felipe Larraín and Andrés Velasco, *Can Swaps Solve the Debt Crisis? Lessons from the Chilean Experience*. (November 1990)
70. Kaushik Basu, *The International Debt Problem, Credit Rationing and Loan Pushing: Theory and Experience*. (October 1991)
71. Daniel Gros and Alfred Steinherr, *Economic Reform in the Soviet Union: Pas de Deux between Disintegration and Macroeconomic Destabilization*. (November 1991)
72. George M. von Furstenberg and Joseph P. Daniels, *Economic Summit Declarations, 1975-1989: Examining the Written Record of International Cooperation*. (February 1992)

SPECIAL PAPERS IN INTERNATIONAL ECONOMICS

15. Gene M. Grossman and J. David Richardson, *Strategic Trade Policy: A Survey of Issues and Early Analysis*. (April 1985)
16. Elhanan Helpman, *Monopolistic Competition in Trade Theory*. (June 1990)

REPRINTS IN INTERNATIONAL FINANCE

24. Peter B. Kenen, *Forward Rates, Interest Rates, and Expectations under Alternative Exchange Rate Regimes*; reprinted from *Economic Record* 61, 1985. (June 1986)
25. Jorge Braga de Macedo, *Trade and Financial Interdependence under Flexible Exchange Rates: The Pacific Area*; reprinted from *Pacific Growth and Financial Interdependence*, 1986. (June 1986)
26. Peter B. Kenen, *The Use of IMF Credit*; reprinted from *Pulling Together: The International Monetary Fund in a Multipolar World*, 1989. (December 1989)
27. Peter B. Kenen, Transitional Arrangements for Trade and Payments Among the CMEA Countries; reprinted from *International Monetary Fund Staff Papers* 38 (2), 1991. (July 1991)